Working Organization Habits

Improve your Productivity and Manage the Organization of your Habits in Order to Make More Time for Yourself

By
Tyler Dolton

DISCLAIMER

This book is writing to help your family get organized. All information is well documented to enable a better lifestyle. Please note that getting involved and practicing all the proven information in this book will requires knowledge and techniques; we have done a lot of research before writing this book.

TABLE OF CONTENTS

INTRODUCTION

Nobody can organize your workspace as adequately as possible. Indeed, even professional organizers (who presently number more than 1000, as per the National Association of Professional Organizers) can't. They can make a structure, and because they charge for their assistance, a great many people attempt to work inside that structure for a period.

If this is valid, is there any desire for you? Unquestionably. You have the benefit of knowing your particular authoritative needs, and that enables you to build up a framework that works for you. Decide your dependable needs first; at that point, organize yourself.

Sound exhausting to you? It is. Not every person can live with an unbendingly organized framework, and not every person should. You need to organize your work with the goal that it addresses your issues, such that it makes you generally productive. On the off chance that flawless little cubbyholes and one after another in order masterminded and marked supplies are what you need, that is fine. A large portion of us, in any case, need to customize how we organize our own and professional lives with the goal that they sound good to us.

In this exercise, you will distinguish your particular authoritative needs by evaluating the specific issues you face at work. The way to making a successful arrangement is to know your qualities and shortcomings; at that point, choose where you have to concentrate.

Where Do You Begin?

How disorganized would you say you are? The majority of us genuinely don't have the foggiest idea of how chaotic we are, because we can, as a rule, but the fault for our pressure and disappointments on any number of other workplace issues. While these may add to our sentiments of being compelled or overpowered, they are infrequently the sole issue, and they regularly vanish once we take control.

It is good to say that you are organized enough to finish a typical office task? Before you answer, think about how your present condition of the association at work would enable you to deal with the accompanying speculative circumstance:

You work for a little organization, where your obligations regularly cover with those of the other three individuals in the workplace. A few activities necessitate that every one of the four individuals works with a similar arrangement of records, while different ventures are taken care of solo. You have recently finished making calls to accumulate insights and cost information to organize the initial period of another experiment that the organization will offer on. Realizing that you had a ton of requests to make and that a portion of the data would be futile, you composed everything down on a lined cushion.

Presently, you're prepared to enter your discoveries on the suitable structures in the venture document organizers before offering them to the individual liable for finishing the following period of the exploration for which your data is required.

What do you do?

a. Get up from your work area, find the suitable organizers in the sequentially orchestrated file organizer cabinet, enter the data, and return the envelopes to their right request in the file organizer
b. Pull open the drawers of your work area, get each document organizer on the work area and check whether it contains the task

materials and sort through heaps of records and different elements that encompass your work area.

c. Ask your coworkers if they have the document and glance through each organizer stacked on their work areas.

d. Give up attempting to find the envelopes that contain the first reports, run duplicates of the structures, name another record organizer, and let another person stress over finding the first envelopes.

Answer an is the perfect circumstance and one that you can make a reality by arranging to manage your particular hierarchical needs. Knowing precisely where the documents are and that they are quickly accessible to you evacuates the pressure and perplexity of looking for them. You anticipate a picture of professional ability and certainty when you essentially pull back the documents as required and enter the data that you worked so tricky to accumulate.

Answer b activities will leave you looking and feeling fatigued, and your professional picture will endure. As you scan wildly for the data on the one anticipate, you will make a significantly more prominent confusion on your work area as you stack and restack papers, documents, folios, and different materials.

Far more detestable, others in the workplace will see your disarray and question your fitness, which can convert into diminished open doors for headway.

Answer c is additionally not attractive because your errand is the principal stage in the undertaking, so you are the primary individual to enter assembled data into the records. The others are sitting tight for your information before they can proceed onward to the later stages, so they needn't bother with the documents until you have entered your data. That being said, in any case, oppose the compulsion to look through another person's work area and papers.

Answer d is enticing, however firmly exploitative and dangerous. The first documents most likely contain the consequences of a primer examination of the task that was ordered by one of the organization chiefs before relegating periods of the exploration to the workplace staff. Even though duplicates of the data are most likely recorded in a few different spots, you must find the organizer with which you were working.

It is good enough to say that you are happy with how your present work circumstance would have enabled you to deal with the above situation?

Do you feel powerful and equipped for taking care of most normal day by day circumstances at work?

On the opportunity that you were accountable for rating your presentation at work, okay, give yourself high checks as a worker?

Do you rate your job fulfillment as high?

A "no" response to at least two of the above questions implies that you are presumably not taking full advantage of your job, and sloppiness is likely the explanation.

CHAPTER 1

WORKING ORGANIZATION HABITS

YOUR MIND AND HABITS TOWARDS WORK

We are altogether destined to have fruitful existences; however, our molding drives us to disappointment. We are destined to win; however, we are adapted to lose. We frequently hear proclamations like this individual is merely fortunate, he contacts earth, and it goes to gold or, he is unfortunate, regardless of what he touches, it goes to the soil. This isn't valid. If you investigate, the fruitful individual is accomplishing something directly in every exchange, and the disappointment is rehashing a similar slip-up in every transaction.

Keep in mind, and practice doesn't make flawless. Just impeccable careful discipline brings about promising results. The method causes perpetual whatever you to do more than once. A few people continue rehearsing their mix-ups, and they become flawless in them. So their slip-ups become impeccable and programmed. Professionals make things look simple since they have aced the basics of whatever they do. Numerous individuals do great work given advancements. Be that as it may, the one to whom a great job turns into a habit is meriting.

Developing a habit resembles furrowing the field. It requires some investment. It needs to grow from inside. Patterns produce different practices. Motivation is the thing that kicks an individual off; the inspiration is the thing that keeps him on track, and habit is the thing that makes it programmed.

The capacity to show fearlessness notwithstanding affliction; show patience despite enticement; pick joy even with hurt; show character despite despair; see opportunity notwithstanding obstructions. These attributes are not fortuitous events; they are the consequence of steady and predictable preparing, both mental and physical. Despite the misfortune, our conduct must be the one we have polished, paying little respect to whether it is individual or negative.

At the point when we practice negative qualities, for example, weakness or unscrupulousness in little occasions, wanting to deal with the significant ones out of a positive way, the last wouldn't occur because that isn't what we have drilled. Achievement lies in the way of thinking of support and avoid.

Support what should be done and refuse what is negative until this gets habitual. People are more passionate than usual. Trustworthiness and respectability are both the aftereffect of our conviction framework and practice. Anything we practice long enough gets imbued into our structure and turns into a habit.

A straightforward individual, more often than not, gets captured on the first occasion when he tells an untruth. Though an individual who is deceptive more often than not gets caught on the first occasion when he comes clean. Trustworthiness and unscrupulousness to self as well as other people both become habits. Our reasoning example gets habitual. We structure habits and habits structure character.

Before you understand that you have the habit, the habit has got you. We have to frame the practice.

Somebody once stated, "Our contemplations lead to activities, activities lead to habits, and habits structure character." Character prompts fate.

What fixes habits?

Habits, positive or negative, are fixed by reiteration and fortification. Everyone knows about the job that reiteration plays inhabit arrangement, yet regularly we neglect to persevere for enough time to make another normal programmed. We have to recall likewise that redundancy will possibly work on the off chance that it is joined by support. Support can be sure or negative. Regularly disregarded instances of uplifting feedback incorporate an expression of compliment (regardless of whether it originates from yourself) or virtually the lift that originates from check a thing of your schedule.

Negative support may come as unwelcome distress. A few reinforces are more grounded than others. Those that are clear and prompt will, in general, have more impact than those that are obscure and later on.

On account of Frances and her work area habits, the outcomes of any unique method for acting are unclear and inconclusive by examination with the prompt support gave by her present work habit, which she sees as the capacity to move rapidly and effectively starting with one job then onto the next with the base of planning or clean-up time.

To change her conduct, she needs to make a voluntary association between various habits and their results and to work on fortifying it each time she shows the ideal manner. Patterns are additionally supported by your condition – including your very own frames of mind and view of self, those near you, and the prevailing culture in your work environment.

Frances' perspective on herself as an occupied, imaginative type is some portion of the foundation to her conduct, similar to the inclination in her workplace to see a vacant work area as a marker of someone with insufficient to do. It pursues from this that choosing you will bring new schedules into your working day is no assurance of progress.

You have to address the earth where your present conduct twists, and work on sustaining and fortifying the ideal habit until it gets programmed. It won't occur quickly, yet the final product will merit a touch of industriousness.

Various things may impede powerful essential leadership:

- fears and tensions;
- accessibility of data and different assets;
- clashing timescales;
- the conduct of others.

Dread

Dread, as we have just observed, is a factor in delaying. Choices are frequently deferred or alluded somewhere else out of fear of committing an error. Nervousness about the way toward actualizing a decision might be similarly as significant as picking the correct strategy.

You may realize what the right activity is, yet the possibility of doing it is terrifying. Perhaps it holds the potential of upsetting experiences with others. Troublesome choices to do with individuals – disciplinary matters, for instance – are regularly kicked consequently.

Data

Data is the reason for supposed 'examination loss of motion.' Either there is insufficient data to settle on an educated choice – regularly an idea used to legitimize lingering – or there is such a lot of that the individual answerable for the decision is overpowered. There is a dread component to data assembling as well.

From one perspective lies the dread that procuring additional data may hurl further entanglements. On the other is the similarly harming apprehension that on the off chance that you stop data gathering, you may miss an essential chunk that would set you destined for success.

You have to keep information procurement about the significance of the issue to be chosen and figure out how to perceive the time when you have acquired adequate information to characterize and gauge the choices satisfactorily, without tipping over into extra work, creating quickly declining advantages.

Timing

You shouldn't be told about lucky chances. Settling on the correct choice at an inappropriate time can be as harming as settling on an inappropriate choice at the ideal time. A few decisions must be taken rapidly, and vacillating will enable the minute to pass. Be that as it may, take care not to surge choices which need cautious thought – maybe because there are a few stages to them, or because they have suggestions for different exercises. There may likewise be short-and long haul measurements to the issue you are thinking about. Taking care of business for a long haul arrangement is, for the most part, to be supported over continued staying mortar reactions.

The conduct of others

Choices are not taken in a vacuum. Generally, they will affect other people who will accompany their full share of biases, pastime steeds, and stuff as the view of status, job, and notoriety. They may be persuaded of the advantages and maybe to take responsibility for the choice. Overlook this, and you should disregard settling on the decision by any means.

There are five sections to settling on any genuine choice:

1. Explain what you are about. This is best cultivated by posing yourself a few inquiries:
   - Why do I have to settle on this choice?
   - What are the objectives I wish to accomplish?
   - What data do I have to settle on this choice?
   - What will occur on the off chance that I don't, isn't that right?
   - Who do I have to include?
   - What is the timescale?
   - What assets are accessible to me?

2. Distinguish the accessible choices. This is a time when short-circuits regularly happen. During the time spent distinguishing options, an externally alluring one springs up, and the center moves from investigation everything being equal and towards supporting why this specific arrangement ought to be picked. Indeed, even with choices that require a fast reaction, it merits requiring some investment to guarantee you have recognized all the potential opportunities before you begin to assess them.

3. Gauge the upsides and downsides of every choice A straightforward methodology is to receive an asset report system for this undertaking. Try not to regard the upsides and downsides as though they all convey equivalent weight. You might need to give each a weighting on, state, a one to ten scales. Yet, recollect that you can't hope to arrive at a resolution just by dispensing and including weightings. A few may have total as opposed to relative noteworthiness. A solitary point against might be of such weight that it wipes out every one of the focuses in support. Be careful additionally of what may appear to overpower aces. The curiosity

estimation of specific alternatives may prompt the cons of not being satisfactorily investigated.

4. Pare the choices down to the indicate that you are capable settle on a decision. A few options will have been promptly rejected by neglecting to meet the objectives or having intense focuses against them. For those that remain, you have to assess hazard encompassing their usage. How likely is it that elements outside your ability to control may influence the effective execution of choice? Furthermore, what is the equalization of hazard against potential addition? Likewise, consider components, for example, how the option will be offered to the individuals who need to actualize it.

5. Sell the result taking the choice may not be the time when the job completes, rather the time when it begins. It is frequently than a matter of conveying the decision and picking up the responsibility of others, and this is the place a ton of good choices unhinge. Carrying the selection is a selling job, and the standards of successful influence apply:

    - Approach the assignment from your crowd's perspective. Address their goals and fears.

    - Establish believability by showing a reasonable arrangement for the usage of choice.

    - Sell the advantages of the choice as opposed to harping a lot on the purposes behind it.

    - Anticipate any protests that might be raised and plan to persuade reactions to them.

Presently proceed onward

Perceive that you can never take care of business regularly, especially when there are individuals included. At the time you settle on the choice, its usage lies later on. Conditions may change for reasons you couldn't have anticipated at the time you decided on the opportunity, and due to that, you do need to hold the outcomes of decisions under audit. Be that as it may, having picked the best alternative, you have to actualize it and proceed onward, without always returning to the choices to stress whether you have settled on the correct decision.

ORGANIZE INFORMATION

- Does the measure of approaching data you are required to manage to appear to be always developing?
- Do you wind up going over a similar material more than once without appearing to take it in?
- Do you experience issues staying up with the latest with the perusing you feel is essential for viable execution of your job?
- Do partners shell you with sent messages, reports, and duplicates of other composed material that you needn't bother?
- Do you get yourself unfit to choose how to manage archives and messages you get?
- Do you put things to the other side to be managed later?
- Do you hold magazines, reports, and web-references meaning to understand them, however, never get around to it?
- Are you tormented by garbage mail?
- Do you discover trouble finding a snippet of data that you know is someplace inside a specific book or report?

On the off chance that you haven't addressed yes to any of these, at that point, you are an entirely different being in the present workplace. We will look at approaches to diminish the volume of what comes to your direction and procedures to enable you to peruse, sort, and acclimatize it all the more productively.

Recognize the significant data

Some data is promptly conspicuous as garbage. Different things shout their significance. Utilize the accompanying inquiries to help decide the estimation of whatever data comes to your direction:

- Does this data identify with a critical component of my job?
- Would I decide to get or keep this data if I needed to pay for it?
- What is the most terrible that would occur if I disregarded it?
- Is it data that I need as of right now. If not, would I be able to get to it effectively? Would it be a good idea for me to need it in the future?
- 80% of the worth originates from 20 percent of the data. Is this thing in the best 20 percent?

You can't make sure of taking care of business unfailingly, yet oppose the impulse to manage this vulnerability by a system of 'if all else fails, treat it as significant.' Data flawlessness – continually having precisely the correct data accessible at the opportune time – is impossible. While the accessibility of useful data is imperative to the successful release of your job, more data won't ensure better execution.

 Past a specific point, extra data will have a declining peripheral worth, and data has no incentive at all if there is such a large amount of it that it can't be appropriately deciphered and comprehended. In this way, perceive you have no desire to take in all things, center around the significant, and acknowledge that your judgment will be flawed. Keep in mind, likewise, the need to separate between the pressing and the substantial.

Things requiring a rapid reaction may accept a more prominent significance than they merit. An irrelevant issue that has been left unattended for a few days doesn't turn out to be progressively significant because it's cutoff time is drawing closer. It essentially turns out to be increasingly earnest.

Embrace a deliberate methodology

There is a typical legend, sustained by some time the board programs, that each thing of data ought to be dealt with just once. It doesn't work like that in reality. For an assortment of reasons, you may need to return to a report. A thing may genuinely be thought about or set up together with other data before you can settle on a reasonable choice upon it. It might be increasingly productive to manage a few things in setting with others on a similar subject. Shouldn't something be said about the report which aggravates you?

Albeit a reaction shot promptly may accomplish something for your circulatory strain, you are probably going to create a progressively compelling answer, and one less inclined to heighten showdown on the off chance that you hold up until you have chilled.

A few things may need continued taking care of during the time spent drafting a perplexing archive. If it is conceivable to contact a file just once, at that point, this is obviously what you should go for; however, don't turn out to be also hung up on the 'one-touch' approach. Guarantee that no record or message returns onto the heap and that each thing gets a positive activity on the central touch.

The snappiest method to get impeded with data is by sitting around idly and vitality perusing material of next to zero advantage to you. Along these lines, the central inquiry to pose to yourself is, 'Do I need this by any stretch of the imagination?' It ought to be rapidly clear if a thing has no utilization for you.

However, we are regularly hesitant to consider the receptacle until we have swum through a record. There is likewise a propensity to put to the other side archives that one is uncertain.

There they structure a mounting heap with different things, gathering residue or obstructing your inbox – at times being returned to in apathetic endeavors to clear the accumulation. A helpful, dependable guideline is – on the off chance that it doesn't appear to be relevant today, it isn't probably going to tomorrow.

Manage

Given that you can do so rapidly and successfully; you should manage things when they initially come to you. A quick activity on a report is fulfilling and stress-relieving. Where it is preposterous to expect to manage a thing promptly, at that point, in any event, figure out what move you will make and when.

Decide future activity

When managing paper, stay away for the indefinite future a thing to the heap. Ensure you have a framework for presenting stuff on which you should act, and try noticing the activity required, or the potential alternatives, on the record or a clingy note connection. A concertina document set apart with the dates of the month makes a helpful 'present' gadget. Spot the thing in the compartment relating to the time when you wish to return to it. Use venture documents for things that should be worked upon with others as a significant aspect of a bigger errand. You can embrace a comparative methodology with messages.

Utilize the 'banner for development' office in Outlook, which enables you to choose the kind of activity required and pick a date on which you will get a reminder. You may likewise need to add a remark to the email to help you in managing it when the opportunity arrives.

Don't just return it to your inbox after you have done this. Spot it in a proper envelope or, if your email programming doesn't have a subsequent reminder, set up an organizer for activities pending and try visiting it routinely.

You should apply some control regarding things decided for future activity:

- Do not utilize it to evade one of the other four Ds.
- Do not move things on past the day you have initially set for activity.
- If you have a 'to peruse' record, don't give it a chance to turn into a general dumping ground.

Direct

Try not to send things to others to get them off your work area or out of your inbox, or because you don't have the foggiest idea how to manage them. You will add to other individuals' data trouble, further dwell on the inside correspondence framework, and potentially fill the canisters of others more rapidly than your own. Consider why you are diverting the thing and what you need the other individual to do with it. A short note will assist them with assimilating and follow up on it more rapidly.

Store

Putting away a thing in whatever type of documenting framework isn't a move to make since you don't have the foggiest idea what else to do with it. Be saving in what you record.

Stay away from over-burden

Anyway compelling you become at taking care of the stuff, you won't accomplish all that is conceivable except if you likewise find a way to diminish the volume of data that every day lands for your consideration. Regardless of whether you look at most of it, you might be burning through exciting time and exertion. The most significant advance you can take is to analyze your conduct.

Your adage must be 'do unto others as you would have them do unto you.' The more your appropriate data superfluously, the more you are probably going to get it consequently.

Here are some different thoughts:

- Don't welcome garbage mail by giving out your subtleties pointlessly. What's more, don't sit around idly on the garbage mail you get. You can dump the lion's share without opening it.
- Remove your name from mailing records on the off chance that they furnish you with nothing of significant worth.
- Consider inward interchanges. Course records inside associations are frequently superfluously enormous. If you can do as such without making political troubles for yourself, request to be left off dissemination records for reports which don't concern you in any capacity.
- Examine memberships to periodicals, ezines, and other online diaries. Those who have not yielded anything beneficial over the most recent a half year might be expected for scratch-off.

Concentrate on what is significant

Sooner or later in many records, there will be deviations from the fundamental contention, things which you know, stuff you don't have to know, and clear cushioning. An ideal approach to move toward any perusing errand is with the inquiry 'What do I need from this?' principal in your mind.

You will peruse all the more rapidly and recall more, on the off chance that you can concentrate on the components which are fundamental for you in whatever assignment you need to satisfy. Try not to move toward the printed word with a lot of worship. The author doesn't have a clue about anything else than you do regarding the matter.

CHAPTER 2

HOW TO ORGANIZE THE WAY
YOU WORK WITH OTHERS?

Quite a bit of our working day is spent on some connection with others. How you approach these associations can considerably affect your viability.

A procedure for gatherings

The time-squandering capability of gatherings is enormous. In numerous associations, you can go through hours consistently in meetings that accomplish practically nothing. Why? Individuals go to gatherings for reasons other than to decide. Groups develop a feeling of one's significance – closeness to the wheels of intensity. They are a chance to establish a connection with your associates. Not being welcomed may liken to prohibition.

I have known individuals, let well enough alone for gatherings that had practically insignificant importance to them, become radiant over what they saw as conscious minimizing endeavors. There is likewise a social component to groups, and they can be less requesting than some different types of work movement.

When you are in the gathering, you're cased, safe from telephone calls, interferences, and the extreme issues that inhabit your inbox. Alright, so groups are exhausting, yet you can play a couple of mind games with partners or let your consideration meander.

For what reason do we hold gatherings? Gatherings are held to:

- Give data;
- Inspire sees;
- Invigorate new thoughts;
- Spur a group;
- Arrive at choices.

There are more successful methods for passing on data than hauling individuals together into a room and exposing them to one of those verbal notice gatherings where just the senior individual talks and every other person sits quietly. There are, likewise, non-meeting methods for counseling and inspiring perspectives.

The imaginative or conceptualizing meeting has, for quite some time, been viewed as a method for investigating new answers for issues. Yet, studies have indicated that now and again, individuals are increasingly innovative when working separately.

Essentially, balanced support and instructing can regularly accomplish more than a persuasive group meeting, and the no challenging society ('mindless obedience') created by specific gatherings may not support great choices.

Along these lines, notwithstanding this, at whatever point the possibility of a gathering comes up, the primary inquiry to pose to yourself is:

Do we need a meeting by any stretch of the imagination? Shockingly that inquiry isn't raised to frequently enough. In numerous associations, gatherings proceed at customary interims paying little respect to whether they are genuinely required.

Business grows to fill the motivation, and you have every one of the elements of exemplary discussing work. Accepting that you choose a gathering truly is fundamental, what would you be able to do to guarantee that it accomplishes its motivation without eating up a lot of the members' time? Inefficient gatherings by and massive tumble down on parts of arranging and the board.

Insufficient arranging

There might be no plan, an ineffectively set one up, or no reasonable reason to the gathering. Data expected to settle on sensible choices might not have been delivered, or members may have neglected to peruse papers given ahead of time.

Poor the board

There might be lacking control of timing, inability to keep discourse on the motivation, powerlessness to control individuals plan on riding their pet leisure activity ponies, failure to coax ends out of the dialog. Here are a few pointers designed for defeating these and other meeting issues.

Ten to recall when assembling a conference

1. Edge the plan as unmistakably as could be expected under the circumstances. Recognize the particular inquiries the gathering needs to address as opposed to setting open-finished subjects.
2. Show an actual time payment for every motivation thing and stick to it as intently as possible.
3. Limit participation to the individuals who have something to contribute to the issues under discourse and the power to execute choices. As a rule, the more individuals there are at a gathering, the more it will take.

4. Calendar gatherings are preceding lunch or by the day's end. Individuals' uneasiness to escape will supersede their verbosity.

5. Do whatever it takes not to plan gatherings in your very own work territory. You will think that its harder to escape from any post-meeting holders on.

6. Start the gathering at the planned time. Sitting tight for newbies urges them to rehash the wrongdoing, and bothers the individuals who have landed on schedule.

7. Try not to enable dialog to be derailed matters, not on the plan. On the off chance that they are significant, they can be managed at a consequent gathering.

8. Try not to sit around talking about issues where there is insufficient data to settle on a choice. Concur duty regarding acquiring and revealing the vital data and delay the dialog to a future date.

9. It is regularly utilized by individuals too apathetic to even think about preparing a thing appropriately for the plan and can bring about terrible choices made based on deficient thought. It can likewise kick into contact with every one of your endeavors at timing discourse.

10. Guarantee that as quickly as time permits after the gathering, a record of the results is readied. The faster it is done, the more straightforward the errand. Itemized minutes are commonly superfluous and give individuals something to contend over toward the beginning of the next gathering. Activity notes are increasingly valuable.

They ought to include:

a) what the meeting concurred;
b) who has duty regarding auctioning those understandings; and
c) dates by which they ought to be actioned.

Ten points recollect when going to a gathering

1. Ensure in advance that you realize what the gathering is planning to accomplish. On the off chance that the point doesn't appear to be clear, question the conveyor about it. This ought to have the impact of explaining goals, prompting an increasingly beneficial gathering, or showing that a group isn't required.

2. Request to be pardoned any gathering, which doesn't seem to have any significance to you. You must be astute to the governmental issues of this. On the off chance that your supervisor is the one assembling the conference, discretion may necessitate that you go. Regularly, be that as it may, the conveyor hasn't given an adequate idea to meeting participation. Questions like 'What are you trusting I will have the option to contribute?' can lead them to reconsider.

3. Ian a gathering applies to you, ask whether it very well may be set close to the start of the motivation with the goal that you can be saved the remainder of the gathering. Know, however, that this strategy, some of the time, starts an offering war concerning others correspondingly influenced.

4. Continuously read the motivation and any papers before a gathering and, without taking up an unbendable position, explain your musings about what you might want to accomplish from the crowd.

5. Your contentions should meet with some restriction, somewhat unpretentious campaigning ahead of time might be valuable. Different members might not have given the gathering a lot of advance thought, and individuals are progressively disposed to stay with a view that they take into the room than they are to be prevailed upon by something they hear during the gathering. Handle campaigning cautiously, however. On the off chance that the other individual considers you to be as an endeavor to apply

disproportionate impact, you hazard dismissing them from your perspective.

6. Ponder what you will agree to if you don't get what you need. A great many people won't have contemplated a fallback position. Skillfully exhibited – that is before it is evident to everybody that you have lost the contention – it very well may be an incapacitating method for getting, at any rate, a generous piece of what you need.

7. Don't overcommit yourself. Gatherings are somewhat similar to barters. In the back and forth of discourse, it's anything but difficult to lose control and make endeavors you later lament. There's a characteristic wish to establish a decent connection before associates, however, don't give yourself a chance to be enticed into taking on an excessive number of duties or offering unreasonable deadlines for the consummation of work.

8. You can help a frail executive by abridging the contentions of others and pulling the strings of a dialog together to encourage choices. By all methods cause people to notice it overwhelms on schedule; however, take care to guarantee that you are not a liable gathering. We will, in general, overestimate the time that other individuals have been talking and belittle our garrulity.

9. Attempt to set some standard occasions when you are accessible for gatherings participation and make them known. If you can make this work, it can help avoid crowds separating your working week so that you can't get to those undertakings which require real action over several hours.

Options in contrast to gatherings

As noted toward the start of this segment, there are progressively effective methods for doing a portion of the business customarily held

24

for gatherings, and these are helped by present-day innovation. A part of the conceivable outcomes is as per the following:

Utilizing email successfully

Dispersal of data to gatherings is speedy and straightforward with email. Viewpoint incorporates instruments like free catches to help meeting or the accumulation of perspectives. These empower members to post issues for discourse, react to the remarks of others, and transfer documents to share.

Texting

As a rule, this can be an immensely aggravating interference to other work; however, as an option in contrast to gatherings, it has significant favorable circumstances, offering as it does straightforward and quick methods for sharing thoughts and responding to questions.

Community-oriented administrations and applications

For action that doesn't require ongoing cooperation, these may give a great workspace wherein notes can be traded, errands allowed, reports shared and worked on cooperatively. There are various administrations accessible – the membership-based PB Works is a model – and a reasonable level of community action is additionally conceivable through free administrations, for example, Microsoft Office Live. Furthermore, some product bundles, for example, venture the executive's applications will likewise take into consideration individuals from a group to work together with a good way off nearly as adequately as though they were getting along.

Video conferencing

This is currently inside the extent of even the littlest business, given the falling expense of required equipment and the accessibility of quick web associations. Where people would somehow or another movement some separation to go to a gathering, the reserve funds in time and travel costs will quickly exceed any arrangement costs. There are heaps of work – individuals whose capability is being extended as far as possible by rivalry, change, and rebuilding.

They are experiencing the dilemma circumstance where they know they should appoint all the more yet feel they haven't an opportunity to do it appropriately. In any case, for anyone who needs to get organized and remain over the job, an appointment must be a piece of the formula. The principal significant point about designation is that it ought not to be an automatic response to your very own over-burden.

It isn't merely an issue of offloading errands you would prefer not to do, however a commitment to generally speaking efficiency by putting duty and the critical position and assets where they can usually be released viably. You will experience issues with assignments in case you're not set up to put the time in setting game plans up, on the off chance that you can't confide in your associates, or if you can hardly imagine how any other individual can carry out the responsibility just as you.

At one time, appointment was found continuously as far as errands being passed to progressively junior associates. Yet, nowadays of compliment authoritative structures, there is an expanded propensity to consider sideways designation – the development of work between partners at the equivalent or a similar level. This is hugely more about exchanging duties than appointing them the conventional sense.

We, as a whole, have different abilities and work inclinations. On the off chance that an associate can satisfy a territory of your obligation more successfully than you, and you like this can carry your abilities to a part of their job, at that point, it bodes well to co-work.

Notwithstanding, the way that the course of action is between partners at a similar level ought not to be a purpose behind any less care in the setting-up process.

Five stages to viable appointment

1. Choose what you will assign The selection of duties to delegate will ordinarily focus on those things that others may accomplish all the more rapidly, more efficiently or more expertly than you, or undertakings that can promptly be performed inside the setting of someone else's current job. There will, for the most part, be central components to your very own job that you ought not to think about appointing.
2. Pick the ideal individual Beware of the characteristic propensity to stack the willing steeds or to delegate undertakings just to the individuals who have satisfied comparative work before. The purposes behind designation are tied in with facilitating your workload as well as about giving new improvement encounters to other people.
3. Set up the ground. You must be prepared to plan partners for what you need them to do. Time to do this is regularly an issue, yet it involves momentary agony for long haul gain. Tell your associate the parameters of their position and what bolster you will have the option to give.
4. Sell the advantages. It's imperative to take a gander at these from the other individual's perspective. There might be preparing, and advancement advantages to the person in question are taking on another obligation, improvement of vocation possibilities, assortment, and challenge, or chance to utilize specific abilities. Beset up to invest energy conversing with the individual concerned, looking for reactions to what you are proposing, and reacting productively. If your associate can fondle that the setting

procedure is a community-oriented one, the individual in question will be progressively dedicated to taking it on.

5. Remain back. Let the other individual continue ahead with it. One of the most widely recognized appointment issues is a propensity to meddle or dismiss the work since it isn't being done in precisely how you would have done it. You have to work hard to maintain a strategic distance from this, especially on the off chance that you have been carrying out the responsibility yourself for quite a while. You should clarify that you are accessible to offer help, yet that everyday obligation is down to the individual to whom you have designated it. On the off chance that you don't, it will remain your obligation, for which you have permanently contracted out a piece of the jackass work. At the point when issues happen, they will end up back on your plate, and your associate won't accomplish the improvement benefits that appointment can offer. The position you agent isn't boundless, and the individual assuming on the liability ought to know about its cutoff points; however, the person in question likewise needs the freedom to work and at times, to commit errors and gain from them.

Beating distractions and interruptions

Interruptions and distractions force intensely on our capacity to organize work plans. Not exclusively is there the real-time lost through the interference be that as it may, all the more significantly, the exertion of returning to the first assignment and re-centering consideration. The degree to which we are occupied from our work has gotten considerably more intense as of late because of innovative advances. We live and work in this present reality where we are always associated, regularly at the same time, to various correspondence vehicles – email, the web, cell phone calls, writings, and texting – also our eye to eye communications with individuals and the effect of antiquated landline media transmission.

In numerous settings, this ever-present connectedness is viewed as a fundamental part of working life, and performing various tasks has become the request for the day. In any case, performing multiple tasks isn't something that individuals are appallingly great at.

We oversee it alright in fact we're worried about exercises that request just negligible consideration. Yet, we think that it's especially increasingly troublesome when occupied with those requiring innovativeness, unique idea, or supported core interest. A concentrate in 2007 led by Microsoft Research and the University of Illinois found that it takes as long as 15 minutes to beneficially continue a troublesome errand when hindered by something as straightforward as an email.

What's more, interruptions can bring about diminished precision of memory as well. They meddle with the matter of preparing data between the present moment and long haul memory. It has been discovered that in certain occupations, workers are exchanging their consideration like clockwork, and the hindering impacts of this are turning out to be so generally recognized that another term – 'consistent halfway consideration disorder' – is progressively used to depict them.

Not all distractions and interruptions are innovative. Some are social, frequently by individuals who are themselves occupied with lingering over undertakings they need to getaway. You may even be the wellspring of the distraction. It is anything but difficult to persuade yourself that you need to make a telephone call, get an espresso, or check your preferred blog, and you will be in the groove again in almost no time.

When the example of work is disturbed, you discover other squeezing errands, and the minutes to an hour or increasingly, at which point it is a lot harder to get the strings. You will always be unable to dispose of interruptions.

Yet, you can do a ton to diminish them, and to make those staying as brief and intentional as could reasonably be expected. Plan to remove all bar the direst and essential – those things that infringe on the principal reason for your job or the association you work for, and where the outcomes of inability to give the issue your prompt consideration might be of disadvantage to either.

The incredible advantage of email, voice message, and content informing ought to be their time autonomy, and you will unquestionably be undeniably increasingly beneficial if you can manage them on occasion based on your personal preference instead of when they show up. Research has indicated that individuals handle messages and different interruptions substantially more successfully on the off chance that they happen at a usual break focuses on different exercises they are completing.

If it is feasible for you to do as such, set a few times every day when you will routinely check and manage calls and messages, and be restrained about adhering to this daily practice. Shockingly for some peruses, this may appear to be an unachievable extravagance. Culture where there is a desire for quick reactions to calls and messages, it might feel practically challenging to free yourself of constant interruptions.

You should think about a methodology that mirrors the triage systems utilized in crisis prescription – sifting through those messages which must be managed promptly from the rest that can hold up until an increasingly advantageous time. One approach to understanding the significant issues rapidly is to set your email programming to download headers instead of the full message.

You diminish the impulse to manage each word quickly if another activity is required before you can understand it, and you can, as a rule, tell which messages are significant from the header data. It's likewise a smart thought to mood killer audible warning of approaching messages and messages. There's nothing bound to make us hinder what we are doing than the dire signal of a showing up news.

You may likewise prefer to consider giving yourself email free periods during the day – times when you can work continuously on undertakings that require your total consideration. In case you're worried about guaranteeing availability for essential messages in any event, during your email free periods, you should seriously mull over setting your email programming to give you an audible or on-screen alert just when messages from specific senders or those containing certain words in the header are gotten.

You may, for instance, let individuals realize that to contact you straight away, they ought to incorporate the word 'quick' in the headline of their message. If you have an automated assistant office, you should seriously mull over setting up a message along the accompanying lines: 'A debt of gratitude is for your message.

I'm occupied on an assignment that requires all my consideration and can't react right away. I check my messages normally and will hit you up today. An elective technique to the utilization of 'rules and alarms' (which won't work if the product is set to download just headers) is to assign a subsequent email address for pressing messages and to set this up for the prompt notice.

Fifteen additional approaches to decrease interruptions

1. Know what you are attempting to accomplish in your day will we help you to rate the significance of distractions and interruptions, and maintain your attention on what makes a difference as far as by and tremendous profitability.

2. Solidify errands, for example, sending messages and making telephone calls to stay away from everyone turning into a different interference to your workflow. You will deal with them all the more viably and spare large measures of time that may right now be spent re-centering after every intervention. 3. Return telephone calls promptly and again when individuals are probably not going to be quick to enter protracted discussions – just before lunch, or toward the day's end when they need to return home. On the other hand, set planned gets back to when consenting to telephone – 'I have five minutes to save between arrangements at four o'clock. Would I be able to telephone you at that point?'

3. Give thorough briefings when passing on undertakings to other people, so they have less need to return to you with follow-up questions.

4. Explain directions and address any shortcomings in methods that lead to rehashed questions, and manage demands rapidly to stay away from individuals pursuing you.

5. Set ordinary occasions every day when you will manage those assignments that require continuous fixation and will be inaccessible for gatherings, calls, and different interruptions. Stick to it unbendingly, and, with karma, others will come to regard your interference-free zone.

6. If you work in an open arrangement condition and have no other method for flagging occasions when you don't wish to interfere, consider utilizing an 'alright to Disturb/Please Do Not Disturb' card by your work area.

7. Help to encourage an atmosphere helpful for viable work by regarding associates as you would have them treat you.

8. Take breaks at foreordained occasions. Incorporate them with a productive work schedule, so they begin to work against self-exacted interruptions.

9. Keep in mind that jumbled workspace is a powerful wellspring of visual distraction. Pursue the counsel in the following part to help decrease any propensity to bounce from undertaking to the task.

10. Consider working from home when you have an errand that necessities concentrated ideas. Given that your home doesn't have its very own distractions, you might have the option to accomplish more in a couple of long stretches of harmony than is conceivable in a bustling workplace.

11. Investigate a proportional course of action with partners whereby you redirect your telephone to other people so they can take messages when you have to work on an undertaking intruded, and you do likewise for them on different occasions.

12. When completing work on the web, be careful with following hyperlinks that lead you to other intriguing, however unessential material.

13. Free yourself from the conviction that you must always be associated with the off chance that you need to work adequately. While there are numerous advantages to the present moment correspondence culture, there are similarly impressive weaknesses. As noted before, viable performing various tasks is, to a great extent, a fantasy. Just by turning off or generally constraining wellsprings of interference for at any rate some portion of your working day, will you have the option to introduce yourself with the space to do undertakings requiring concentrated consideration?

Keeping interruptions brief and profitable

At the point when interruptions are unavoidable, plan to make them as short as would be prudent. Here are a few thoughts:

1. Put a period limit on the interference. Let the individual interfering with you realize that you can just extra, say, five minutes. A few specialists recommend keeping an egg clock around your work area and utilizing it to remind your guest to arrive at the point rapidly.
2. Hazard being viewed as impolite by not welcoming interrupters to plunk down.
3. Position office furniture and work area to abstain from giving your working region a ', please stroll in and plunk down' appearance.
4. Urge partners to accompany a visual cue note of what they need to converse with you about. This causes you to tune into the issue rapidly, encourages them to center their thinking, and prevents progressively unnecessary interruptions on account of the readiness in question.
5. Making interruptions to inference and sending guests on their way, consider your non-verbal communication and the verbal signals inside a discussion that enables you to wrap the gathering up without unduly irritating the other individual.

Help other people to be increasingly organized

Regardless of everyone, organize your calendar and method for working, the disruption of others can even now toss you into perplexity, so it merits giving some consideration regarding techniques for more prominent association among everyone around you.

Disorganized associates

Addressing individuals on their sloppiness will only here and there lead to substantially more than hesitant consistency, and, as none of us are complete without flaw, it will regularly be joined by secretly traded protests of, 'He/she's a fine one to talk.' Getting individuals to verbalize their very own troubles and the strategies they can embrace to determine them is probably going to be unmistakably increasingly beneficial. This is commonly a matter of posing the correct inquiries in a setting that empowers reflection – a coordinated gathering or evaluation, for instance.

Help your associates to concentrate on each thing in turn, and give quick uplifting feedback as acclaim and consolation when you see them working to alter their way of living. Support is an extremely incredible inspiration for change, so don't hold up until the adjusted conduct hits you between the eyes. Effectively search for things to adulate.

Friend weight can likewise be a substantial effect in a singular manner. It might merit thinking about whether there is mileage in an entire group activity planned for working towards improved viability.

Disorganized chief

A disorganized supervisor can be a bad dream to work for, yet don't treat their shortcomings just as a problem to be imparted to different partners over espresso. If you go about it the correct way, you can have any effect; however, you should be substance to work on those parts of your manager's conduct that you can impact, and endure those you can't.

Ensure that your very own work and association can't be blamed, and stay away from full-frontal challenges except if you have another job to go to. Here are five qualities as often as possible showed by disorganized managers with proposals on what to do about them.

Failure to settle on a choice

Keep in mind that supervisors are only occasionally bosses of their predetermination. As opposed to smoking over what may appear from the start sight to be hesitation and antagonism, endeavor to comprehend the legislative issues wherein they are working, and give them the ammo to face conflicts further up the line.

Perceive likewise that your manager may experience issues checking out an issue, which has been the focal point of your consideration for quite a long time or even weeks. Beset up to talk through the manners of thinking, which have prompted the ends you have come to.

An inclination towards on the spot judgment calls

This species lies at the opposite finish of the scale from the ambivalent chief and will manage any inquiry by conveying top-of-the-head sureness's. Anything that likens to thinking time or thought of options is for weaklings. Never approach such a supervisor with an open-finished inquiry, except if you need to wind up burdened with unworkable arrangements and unimaginable cutoff times.

Work out the alternatives already and present them with a pertinently contended thumbnail control. The supervisor will regularly need to be credited with a choice, so work in at any rate one point where there is a decision to be made between options, neither of which would be heartbreaking.

Powerlessness to end gatherings

On the off chance that your manager is the individual who thinks that its hard to close a gathering, ensure that you have another squeezing commitment, which permits you a getaway course inside a reasonable time.

Inability to set clear targets or spotlight on the significant issues Clarify your points and destinations by recording what you think they are and getting your supervisor to affirm them. In balanced gatherings with your chief, give a composed rundown of the issues for discourse and rundown potential answers for problems.

Failure to recall what the individual in question has requested that you do

Build up an act of taking notes at whatever point you meet to examine assignments, and sending your manager an activity notes itemizing what you have consented to do, as quickly as time permits a while later.

Figure out how to state 'no.'

An enormous piece of sorting out yourself is tied in with staying responsible for your workload. If you generally state 'yes' to demands that come to your direction, at that point, you lose that control.

Your over-trouble yourself, with the resultant pressure, and by saying 'yes' too insignificant solicitations, you may get yourself unfit to satisfy critical goals.

There are various reasons why saying 'no' might be troublesome:

- You would prefer not to seem reluctant and ruin your possibilities.
- You're worried that you may disappoint others or hurt their emotions.
- You think little of the expanded weight you will be under because of saying 'yes.'
- You don't understand that adage 'no' is a choice.

You would prefer not to get notoriety for cynicism – an automatic 'no' might be more terrible than an automatic 'yes.' If you are setting up yourself in a new position or intrigue gathering, you may need to state 'yes' more frequently than is beneficial for you.

In any case, it is critical to have the option to adhere to a meaningful boundary skillfully and confidently and perceive that it is difficult to satisfy everybody continually.

Choose which solicitations you have to turn somewhere near asking yourself:

- How does this fit with my primary goals?
- Will my possibilities be influenced if I don't do it?
- What else may I have to drop or defer to embrace this?
- What will be the impact of that on different destinations?
- Will doing it bring about any adverse way of life impact – altogether expanded pressure, irrational interruption on my recreation time?
- Will I pass up any chance to build up another aptitude on the off chance that I don't do this?

Tentative approach

Reacts to the solicitation with muttered endeavors to defer a choice. Leaves the individual making the solicitation hazy about whether 'yes' or 'no' has been said. Squanders vitality fussing about the tender and winds up doing it angrily.

Self-assured approach

Demonstrates delight at being asked, yet clarifies compactly and cordially why the person can't react emphatically. Recommends conceivable elective methods for completing the errand, and determines what bolster the individual in question can offer to whoever takes on the assignment.

The third is the methodology you should go for. The individual making the solicitation is under no misunderstanding about your reaction or the purposes behind it, yet doesn't leave away from experience irate and bullied, and you don't harm your notoriety for supportiveness and positive thinking.

Take specific consideration with demands where the responsibility asked of you isn't quick, yet comes sooner or later – a solicitation to make an introduction at a meeting, for instance. At the point when the occasion is three months away, it's anything, but difficult to be and command over arranging are the approaches to guarantee that you don't fall into this snare.

CHAPTER 3

ORGANIZE YOURSELF AT HOME AND AWAY

A study led in 2005 assessed that 5 million workers in the UK (just about 20 percent of the workforce) invest some energy working at home or progressing, and anticipated a fast ascent in that figure over the following decade as portable innovation keeps on diminishing the requirement for fixed work areas and inflexible working hours. In the twenty-first century, no book on close to the home association would be finished without thought of the extraordinary difficulties that are working from home or out and about presents.

Working from home

The scope of working from home plans stretches out from those working all day in an independently employed ability to those for whom an incidental episode of home working is a chance of getting away from the distractions of the workplace.

Yet, for every one of the individuals who invest a lot of energy working from home, the authoritative favorable circumstances and troubles are genuinely comparable.

Favorable circumstances:

- Authority over your calendar;
- No one investigating your shoulder;
- Freedom from some workplace distractions;
- Adaptability to space recreation or individual action into what might typically be viewed as working hours.

Troubles:

- Nonattendance of typical workplace structures;
- Absence of supporting associates – may need to shuffle various jobs;
- Potential new distractions;
- The nonappearance of limits among work and home life;
- Workspace constraints.

You will wish to amplify the favorable circumstances and limit the hindrances. Every one of the focuses made before in the book about overseeing time and understanding how you work will be of hugeness. In any case, there are other issues explicit to home working regarding parity, center, and workspace association, which we may helpfully take a gander at now.

Parity

Perhaps the most concerning issue for home-based working is keeping up harmony among work and recreation. You are responsible for your calendar, however except if you take care to define and keep up limits on your working day, you can look for some employment starting to attack all your waking hours and, without a level of order, the work you do may not be exceptionally beneficial. With every one of the trappings of your home around you, there might be a propensity to flutter between work errands and relaxation/family action in a way that diminishes the viability of your work and, given blame about ignored work undertakings, doesn't allow full pleasure in recreation exercises.

To keep up a reliable and profitable harmony among work and relaxation, assemble a structure to your working day. It might be useful to see your day as far as center time and adaptable time utilizing a more extensive way to deal with the standard flextime guideline.

41

The center time is what will consistently be allotted to work or family/recreation movement – no reason, this time is consecrated. For instance, you may choose that from 8.30 am until 1.30 pm consistently is center working time and the period after 6.30 pm is center recreation time. The adaptable time to make up your working week can move to oblige a stable recreation balance.

One day may include an early morning start, another first night work, and a third may pursue conventional available time. If you have a massive square of working time that gets standard and that your family, companions, and customers can tune into, you can exploit the adaptability that working from home ideas to improve your way of life.

Equalization additionally includes in the manner you structure your working hours to guarantee you get the best out of yourself and give satisfactory regard for the various parts of your work. You have to concentrate not just on those center exercises that acquire the cash, yet on the support undertakings as well: those routine jobs that keep you working appropriately – remaining educated, managing correspondence, and arranging your workspace. In a conventional work setting, there are probably going to be others whose master jobs support your own.

The odds are that when you are working from home, it's everything down to you. Just as satisfying your first job, you may find that you are going about as your office supervisor, PA, accountant, promoting official and unspecialized temp job individual. It might be impracticable or uneconomic to utilize others in these limits; thus, you have to discover ways by which the full scope of action required for progress will be accomplished.

As opposed to enabling errands to develop until you are compelled to have an accounting spend too much or a recording rush, produce a fluctuated work timetable to impart easy habits by meshing the various jobs into your day by day or week by week schedule.

Ask yourself the accompanying inquiries:

- What are the different jobs I have to satisfy? (Show them.)
- Roughly what extent of my time will be taken up by each of these?
- How does the market rate for these jobs contrast and the value every hour that I would put on my time in my first job?

At the point when you are clear about the appropriate responses, you may jump at the chance to consider a proper working course of action to guarantee the vital administrations are satisfied. Additionally, you may go about as a general executive for thirty minutes consistently. Imagining your various situations along these lines can assist you with getting to grasps with them all and keep some from being underestimated or neglected. Putting a cost on the different jobs causes you to understand those errands that may bode well to agreement out.

Core interest

Who reminds you about things that should be finished? Who keeps your inspiration high and assists when you hit a precarious work issue? It's likely all down to you by and by. In any case, time and workload association can assist make with increasing for the nonappearance of partners and tutors:

- It's much progressively significant when you are working individually to design your exercises over various periods, to set evident, reasonable difficulties, and to separate long haul ventures into littler lumps. It makes assignments simpler to deal with and gives you that genuinely necessary feeling of progress.

- Stay over your calendar by whatever means suits you – paper-based or electronic – yet stick to one straightforward framework.
- Consider utilizing agendas of day by day and week after week schedule errands, so nothing gets missed.
- Break up your week with exercises that include human contact, and find a way to fabricate and keep up your networks. Confinement is a continuous issue for those working from home. Other individuals also connected with can give genuinely necessary exhortation and backing.

Fitting workspace

Thoughtfulness regarding the significant association of your workspace can give a massive lift to profitability. Firing off messages from the solace of your bed or mapping out your strategy on a sun-doused porch might be alluring and, in reality, there might be undertakings that you can satisfy quickly and successfully in capricious settings; however, the probability is that for a noteworthy part of your work, some office space is an absolute necessity.

Your home office doesn't need to be excellent – overlook those excessive Sunday supplement changes – yet it ought to be agreeable and useful with consideration paid to a design that suits your working needs.

Over and over again, we disregard, in our home working game plans, includes that we would view as necessary if we were working somewhere else.

We give ourselves lacking or wrong space and utilize the furnishings and hardware that is to hand instead of investing a limited quantity of energy and cash, making a working situation that meets our prerequisites.

Assess the proposals and think about the accompanying principal components:

- An entryway you can close when vital. Working on the lounge area table might be helpful; however, it displays a pressing up task each time you finish work for the afternoon. It may likewise render you increasingly open to interference if other family unit individuals are available. Maybe above all, it builds the trouble of isolating working life and home life.

- A proportional and movable seat. Regularly disregarded, this is presumably the most significant speculation you will make.

- A work surface that is adequately open to suit essential gear and gives you a lot of free space. It doesn't need to be an extravagant work area; there are a lot of economic, well-structured models accessible, and even foldaway alternatives that could be considered on the off chance that you are working in a multifunction region.

- Working in a dirty box room, encompassed by heaps of garbage, affects your work sooner or later.

- Adequate stockpiling hardware. Racks and stackable boxes may compensate for a deficiency of floor space.

There will be different components to consider, contingent upon the idea of your work. If it includes customers visiting you, what kind of room do you need to get them, and are there any nearby business limitations or agreements that could prompt trouble?

If a lot of your work is done on the phone, do guests consistently get an expert reaction, and might it merit introducing a second line with independent voicemail offices? A subsequent range can likewise be an essential method for guaranteeing that work and recreation don't cover.

Set the work line to get voicemail during your relaxation time and also do with the home line during your working hours. There are different issues – legitimate, commercial, administrative – that may become possibly the most crucial factor with home working game plans, mainly if your exercises include the work of others, premises change, or the setting up of space to be entirely and only utilized as an office. Be that as it may, such issues are past the extent of this book.

There are various books and web destinations, offering valuable data and counsel. Whatever the idea of your locally situated work, go out of the way to explain your needs, inquire about any territories of vulnerability, and organize yourself in like manner.

Sorting out yourself away from the workplace

If your work takes you usually out and about, you will be comfortable with the organizational difficulties such action presents. For you, it involves keeping over your calendar, keeping up compelling correspondence with your base, and guaranteeing that data you need is to hand and that hardware doesn't allow you to down. You share a portion of the difficulties of parity and center that are looked at by those working from home.

Notwithstanding, this area is coordinated less at the individuals who are consistently out and about and are acquainted with the requests of portable working as at all of us, for whom an outing ceaselessly from the workplace is a progressively intermittent occasion and one that may flag significant interruption.

Excursions for work and gatherings can place a massive spanner in your organization's practices. In the hours preceding your takeoff, you end up rushing around to finish errands that won't hold up until your arrival. You at long last figure out how to escape, depleted, and ratty, possibly to find when you get to your goal that you have abandoned an indispensable archive.

Throughout your outing, you are hassled by messages identifying with a minor emergency, goals of which are subject to a snippet of data that sneaks someplace in your documenting framework. At long last, you land back, depleted, troubled with new work, and confronting a build-up of correspondence, voicemail, and email messages.

The way to holding your harmony, when action removes you from the workplace for quite a long time at once, is excellent arranging and adherence, at every possible opportunity, to typical schedules.

Arranging

Build some space into your calendar.

Scale back on any non-critical work in a couple of days preceding your takeoff with the goal that you can focus on those assignments that must be finished before your arrival. Continuously permit more opportunity for this than you might suspect you will require.

Cover your command post.

Guarantee that you have someone who can check your mail, handle any minor emergencies, and discover their way around your recording framework and the data on your PC. Reach numbers.

Check and twofold watch that you have all that you require for the excursion.

Try not to be enticed to take bunches of paperwork in the vain expectation that you will discover time to manage it. You will undoubtedly return with more than you considered.

Put together an 'out of office pack.'

This ought to include everyday extras – envelopes, smaller than expected staplers, pens, adding machines, and so on. Keep this convenient so you can drop it into your attaché when you have an outing to make.]

If you have various areas to visit, plan the request to limit voyaging time. Venture arranging PC programming might be of help with this.

Make sure that you realize how to complete any new assignments.

These incorporate grabbing your voicemail messages remotely, getting an email using the web, or taking advantage of your organization's network while out and about. Don't merely trust directions from another person. Check the activity for yourself before you leave, to guarantee it works. There is nothing more awful than expecting that you will have the option to keep in contact and afterward finding that you can't.

In particular, ensure that you have any passwords you have to get to the previously mentioned offices.

Change your message and set up an email automated message with the goal that guests realize you are away and when you will be back. Incorporate a versatile number if suitable. Make sure to change these messages when you return.

Check that you have all that you need to be introduced on your PC phone — for instance, all significant programming, reference, and contact material. The limit and availability of the modern, versatile PCs imply that you ought to have the option to oblige a similar degree of data as exists on your work area PC.

If you are utilizing an open vehicle, reserve a few errands that are especially fitting for culmination while voyaging. Typically, this will mean chores that are not dependent on significant paper rearranging and can endure some level of interference.

Don't think little of the crippling impact of the movement. Permit some breathing space in your calendar before pitching into gatherings and arrangements.

If your outing includes foreign travel, watch that you have every one of the connectors and rechargers, you have to keep your hardware in a hurry. Ensure likewise that your cell phone is set up to get brings in the nation or nations you are visiting.

If your workstation is set consequently to download updates to its working framework, security programming, or applications, you may need briefly to impair this office. It very well may be disappointing, and possibly very costly, to wind up in the center of an extensive download when you wish to check your messages during a brief stop at an air terminal or web hotspot.

CHAPTER 4

HOW TO STRUCTURE GOOD HABITS
TOWARDS YOUR WORK

The more significant part of our behavior is habitual. It comes naturally without intuition. Character is the

The aggregate of our habits. An individual with negative patterns is a negative character. Practices are significantly more grounded than rationale and thinking. Habits start by being too feeble to even think about being felt and wind up getting too solid to even think about getting out of. Patterns can be created as a matter of course or assurance. I recall as a youngster my folks letting me know, "You should frame great habits since habits structure.

How Do We Form Habits?

Anything we do over and overturns into a habit. We learn by doing. By carrying on fearlessly, we gain courage. By rehearsing trustworthiness and reasonableness, we become familiar with these qualities. By repeating these characteristics, we ace them. So also, if we practice negative aspects, for example, untruthfulness, out of line behavior, or absence of control, that is the thing that we got the hang of. Frames of mind are habits. They are behavior designs. They become a perspective and direct our reactions.

Molding

A large portion of our behavior comes because of molding it is habitual. On the off chance that we need to do anything admirable, it must get programmed. In the event that we need to intentionally consider making the best choice we will always be unable to do it well. That implies we should make it a habit.

We are for the most part being molded ceaselessly by the earth and the media, and we start acting like robots. It is our duty to condition ourselves in a positive way.

At the point when I was an understudy of hand to hand fighting, I saw that even the dark belts were rehearsing square punch, the nuts, and bolts, in such a case that they expected to utilize these aptitudes, they needed to come consequently.

Great habits are difficult to find; however, pure to live. Negative behavior patterns come simple yet are challenging to live with

HOW DO WE GET CONDITIONED?

Think about the compelling elephant who can lift more than a considerable amount of weight with merely its trunk.

How would they condition the elephant to remain in one spot with a feeble rope and a stake?

The elephant, when it is an infant, is attached to an unbroken chain and a stable tree. The infant is powerless; however, the chain and tree are unbroken. The infant isn't accustomed to being tied. So it continues pulling and pulling the chain, all futile.

A day comes when it understands that all the pulling and pulling won't help. It stops. Presently it is adapted. What's more, when the infant elephant turns into the strong mammoth elephant, he is tied with a feeble rope and a little stake. The elephant could, with one pull, leave free, yet it goes no place since it has been adapted.

Individuals are always being adapted, consciously, or unconsciously, by presentation to:

- The sort of books we read;
- The sort of motion pictures and tv programs we watch;
- The sort of music we tune in to;
- The sort of organization we keep.

While heading to work, on the off chance that we tune in to similar music consistently for a few days, and if the cassette player separates, think about what tune we will murmur?

Craziness is characterized as doing likewise again and again and anticipating various outcomes.

If you continue doing what you have been doing, you will keep getting what you have acquired.

The most troublesome thing about changing a habit is unlearning what isn't working and realizing positive habits.

THE GIGO PRINCIPLE

The PC expression GIGO (trash in, trash out) is sound.

Cynicism in; antagonism out.

Inspiration in; energy out.

High in; great out.

Our information rises to our yield. Our subconscious mind doesn't segregate. Whatever we decide to place into our subconscious mind it will acknowledge, and our behavior will mirror that as needs are.

The TV considerably affects impacting our ethics, thinking, and culture, for positive or negative. Television, while getting heaps of valuable data, has additionally made an exceptional commitment to debasing our preferences, adulterating our ethics, and expanding adolescent wrongdoing. That is a significant expense for alleged free discourse or free TV. The number of savage acts seen on TV by the age of 18 tops 200,000.

Publicists are great at molding their group of spectators. Ads sell items, generally for what reason would organizations publicize? At the point when we sit in front of the TV or tune in to a radio commercial, our conscious mind isn't tuning in, yet our subconscious is open, and we get anything that is being dumped in. Have you at any point contended with the TV? Not!

At the point when we go out to see the films, we chuckle, and we cry. Is it since they placed something in the seats or because the passionate information has a quick, enthusiastic yield? Change the data, and the return changes.

THE CONSCIOUS AND SUBCONSCIOUS MIND

Keep in mind, our conscious mind can think. It can acknowledge or dismiss. Be that as it may, the subconscious acknowledges, it sees no difference in regards to enter. On the off chance that we feed our minds with contemplations of dread, uncertainty, and despise, the auto-proposals will initiate and interpret those things into the real world.

The subconscious is the information bank. Of the two, the psyche is all the more dominant. The subconscious resembles the vehicle, while the conscious resembles the driver. The power is in the car; however, the control is with the driver.

The subconscious mind can work possibly in support of us. It isn't sound. At the point when we are not active, we have to reinvent the subconscious.

The subconscious mind resembles a nursery; it couldn't care less what you plant. It is nonpartisan; it has no inclinations. However, on the off chance that you plant high seeds, you will have a decent nursery; else, you will have a wild development of weeds.

I'd go above and beyond to state, in any event, when you plant high seeds, weeds still develop, and the weeding procedure must proceed always.

The human mind is the same. Keep in mind, positive and negative musings can't consume the memory at the same time. Organizations spend near a million dollars for a 30-second advertisement during a significant occasion.

They are getting results. We see a promotion for a specific brand of soda or toothpaste, and we go to the general store and purchase that brand.

We don't need any soda pop; however, just that brand. Why? Since we are modified and act in like manner. To succeed, we have to get customized positively.

HOW DO WE GET PROGRAMMED?

Think about how we figured out how to ride a bicycle. There are four phases: The principal organizes called unconscious ineptitude. This is where we don't have the foggiest idea about what we don't have the foggiest idea. The kid doesn't have a clue what it is to ride a bicycle (unconscious), nor would he be able to ride a bike (ineptitude). This is the phase of unconscious inadequacy.

The subsequent stage is called consciously clumsy. This is where the kid develops and gets conscious of what it is to ride a bicycle yet can't ride one himself, so he is consciously bumbling.

However, at that point, he begins learning, and now comes a third stage, which is called consciously equipped. Presently he can ride a bicycle yet needs to think each opportunity to do it. So with all the conscious ideas and exertion, the kid is skilled in riding a bike.

The fourth stage is called unconsciously competent. It comes when the kid has drilled consciously riding the bike, so a lot of that he doesn't need to think. It turns into a programmed procedure. He can converse with individuals and wave to other people while riding.

That implies he has arrived at the phase of unconscious capability. At this level, we needn't bother with the focus and thinking because the behavior design has gotten programmed. This is the level that we need all our positive habits to reach.

Sadly, we have some negative patterns, too, which are at the unconscious ability to arrange and are impeding our advancement. Studies have demonstrated that roughly 90% of all smokers became smokers by the age of 21.

This demonstrates smoking is molded subconsciously, and our molding begins at a young age.

NATURE ABHORS A VACUUM

I have two nephews matured 12 and 14 who are tennis buffs. One day their dad said to me, "This game is getting over the top expensive. The young men experience the rackets, balls, garden expenses, and now they have a mentor. Everything costs cash." So I asked him, "It is getting costly contrasted, and what?" He could have them quit playing tennis and set aside some cash.

When he stopped to think discreetly for quite a while and afterward stated, "I figure I will have them proceed. It is less expensive along these lines." He understood the significance of keeping them associated with positive exercises. Else they would be pulled in to the negative since nature detests a vacuum. We may have a positive, or we have a negative; there is no impartial ground here.

Character building turns into a habit. Try to construct a satisfying character, we need to analyze our patterns intently. What starts as a periodic guilty pleasure transforms into a lasting defect?

Ask yourself the accompanying inquiries:

1. Do you let the nature of your work fall apart?
2. Do you enjoy the tattle?
3. Are jealousy and inner self a steady partner?
4. Is sympathy hard to come by?

We could continue endlessly. We are animals of habit. It is excellent that it is that way provided that

We need to think before busy continually; we could never complete anything. There is sufficiently not time.

We control our habits by practicing control and self-restraint over our considerations. We have to outfit the intensity of the subconscious mind. We have to develop the habits during youth which assemble character in adulthood.

Plant the correct things right off the bat throughout everyday life. In any case, it is never past the point where it is possible to begin. Each presentation to a positive or negative has any kind of effect. Adapting new habits requires some serious energy yet positive habits, when aced, shine a different light on life.

Optimism or pessimism is a habit. Habits involve the torment and joy principle. We accomplish things either to stay away from pain or to pick up joy. Since the addition is more than the suffering, we proceed with the habit.

For instance, when the specialist advises the smoker to stop, he answers, "I can't! It is a habit and me

Appreciate it!" and he continues smoking. Here the delight is more prominent than the agony.

Until one day, he is looked at a significant therapeutic issue, and the specialist says, "You better stop.

Smoking quickly if you need to live," and he stops. Here the torment is more noteworthy than the delight.

PROTECTION FROM CHANGE

At the point when individuals perceive or become mindful of their negative habits, for what reason don't they

The explanation they don't change is because they won't acknowledge duty. Also, the delight of proceeding is more prominent than the torment.

They may:

- Lack of the longing to change
- Lack of order to change

- Lack of the conviction that they can change
- Lack of mindfulness for the need to change

Every one of these variables keeps us from disposing of our negative habits. We, as a whole, have a decision.

We can overlook negative behavior and expectation it will leave - the ostrich approach- - or face ready and beat it forever. Behavior adjustment originates from defeating unreasonable feelings of trepidation and escaping the safe place. Keep in mind, dread is a learned behavior and can be unlearned.

The accompanying reasons are the most widely recognized clarifications for not changing negative habits:

1. We have always done it that way.
2. We have never done it that way.
3. That isn't my activity.
4. I don't figure it will have any effect.
5. I'm excessively occupied.

CHAPTER 5

SHAPING POSITIVE HABITS THAT EMBRACE WORK LIFE

Notwithstanding our age or how old the habit has been, this should be possible by mindfulness and utilizing procedures that change behavior. We always hear that you can't impart new practices when old ones are so deeply ingrained. We are individuals, not hounds. Nor are we performing stunts. We can unlearn foolish behavior and learn decisive action.

The mystery of fruitful individuals is that they structure the habit of accomplishing things that disappointments don't prefer to do and won't do. Consider the things that disappointments don't prefer to do.

They are very similar things that fruitful individuals don't care to do; however, they do them at any rate. For instance, disappointments don't care for discipline, challenging work, or keeping responsibilities.

Fruitful individuals additionally hate discipline, challenging work (a competitor doesn't care for and need the control to get up and train each day, yet he does it in any case); however, they do it at any rate since they have framed the habit of accomplishing things that disappointments don't care to do.

All habits fire little yet ends up inevitably being very hard to break. Frames of mind are habits and can be changed. It is an issue of getting out from under and supplanting old negative habits with new and positive ones.

It is simpler to forestall negative behavior patterns than to conquer them. Great habits originate from conquering enticement. Satisfaction and despondency are a habit.

Greatness is the consequence of rehashed conscious exertion until it turns into a habit. It needs enough practice to turn into a habit. We, as a whole, have some negative patterns that are pulling us down. Take 15 minutes alone and undisturbed to make a rundown of all the negative habits that are dragging you down. Comprehend how you work.

Calendar assignments at suitable occasions

Almost certainly, your workload comprises of a wide range of assignments. You will have constrained locale over when to complete those that are reliant on the accessibility of others. Yet, for most of the undertakings, there will be some adaptability on timing. Most assignments will be categorized as one of three general gatherings:

- Upkeep assignments – those standard employments which are fundamental to keep you working appropriately, remaining educated, managing the ordinary inflow and outpouring of data, sorting out your workspace, finishing routine correspondence;
- Individuals errands – arranging, taking an interest in gatherings, convincing, evaluating execution, networking, settling protests, introducing, preparing, meeting;
- Innovative, arranging, and critical thinking errands – planning plans and undertaking briefs, composing reports, examining data and making determinations, discovering answers for issues, creating new thoughts.

These are only a couple of models. Contingent upon the nature of your activity, there will be others suitable to you.

Perceive the requests that various errands place on you

As a rule, the upkeep undertakings will make the most restricted vitality requests. Later in this part, we will take a gander at what number of them can be made even less requesting by bridling the intensity of habit. Innovative arranging and critical thinking errands will ordinarily require the best measure of real consideration and bigger squares of time as a result of the need to get yourself up to speed before you can gain vast ground. Individuals errands might be of long or brief length, yet are now and again the ones who make the best requests on passionate vitality.

Those that may include a component of encounter are especially depleting. On the off chance that you have a few of these assignments, take a stab at handling them together – consistently. The head of steam you develop to control the main helps you through the ensuing ones, and, by and large, you will think that its less sincerely depleting than designing yourself up for everyone separately. We are generally acquainted with the possibility of a body clock that directs our dozing and waking.

Anyone who has ever worked a night move or crossed time zones will vouch for the ruin brought about by its interruption. Be that as it may, we give substantially less consideration regarding the pinnacles and troughs of sharpness that happen all through our conscious existence, and which shift fundamentally between people.

The sharpness cycles in your day can potently affect execution, and it pays to plan your most requesting undertakings on the occasions you are best ready to manage them.

What are your best occasions?

We are familiar with depicting ourselves all in all terms – 'I'm a morning individual,' 'I do my best work at night' – however, have you at any point taken a gander at your work designs in more than the most careless terms? You may have become secured in a method for working not especially fit to your body rhythms because of challenges in sorting out your day. You may accept, for instance, that nighttime's are the occasions when you do your best arranging and critical thinking movement, when in certainty those undertakings have been pressed into that day's end since you have thought that it was difficult to give them the concentrated idea they require in the midst of the interruptions and interferences of ordinary working hours.

If, because of better organization, you can bargain all the more viably with interventions, you may find that you can readdress your suspicions about the best occasions to take on specific assignments. Start by analyzing how you presently work with some essential investigation. Record your everyday movement every day for seven days. This can appear as your day by day schedule, enhanced by those other routine exercises that make up your day.

Imprint everything with three images:

1. A letter to show the kind of errand: 'm' for upkeep, 'p' for individuals, 'c' for innovative;
2. Number somewhere between 1 and 5 to show the hour of the day you did it: 1 = early morning, 2 = late morning, 3 = early evening, 4 = late evening, 5 = evening;
3. Plus, or less signs to show apparent vitality levels: ++ = high vitality, + = moderate vitality, – = genuinely low vitality, – = very low vitality.

Toward the week's end, inspect the results to see whether there is an example of a movement that warrants a change. Are there dangerous assignments you are presently endeavoring at seen low spots in your day? Are there simple support errands that would all the more conveniently involve those weak spots? Make changes by your calendar in the next week and note any upgrades in execution.

Why you can't generally depend on similar body rhythms

Your typical example of vitality tops is a decent manual for the occasions when you should plan your most requesting undertakings, yet don't view it as reliable. When you are somewhat sick, or toward the finish of a debilitating week, there might be no calculable vitality tops, and any requesting action is a battle. In these conditions, you are probably not going to get through into bright fields. Obviously, better to change to a progressively usual upkeep undertaking and come back to the serious one when you are refreshed and reenergized.

Be careful, notwithstanding, of utilizing this as basically a reason for lingering. On the switch side of the coin, when things are going exceptionally well, don't stop since you have arrived at the present objective. Keep your timetables adaptable and be set up to tune in to your body.

Fit the undertaking to your accessible time

There are a few undertakings that you can set about if you have a massive lump of time – you have to assemble assets around you, get yourself into the right mood, and ensure that you are free of interferences. Different errands, you can plunge all through more rapidly.

Try not to burn through your time, attempting to prepare for a long-opening assignment when you have a short space accessible. Keep some fast pay-off errands convenient for those extra minutes when someone due for an arrangement is running late, when a gathering doesn't begin on schedule, or while you are hanging tight for a train.

Keep up fixation and inspiration

Our ability for continued focus will change as indicated by the nature of the assignment, the hour of the day, and the level of interruption, however even under the most favorable circumstances it is limited.

While handling large, rationally concentrated undertakings, we need regular breaks that enable us to keep up our core interest. In any case, as we have just noticed, it's anything but difficult to slip into disorganized habits, whereby breaks become preoccupations that take on their very own energy and anticipate us returning to the fundamental undertaking close by.

Expertly arrange your way through protracted assignments by receiving the accompanying standards:

1. Make breaks short and sensibly visit, yet never take them on the drive.
2. Set yourself a progression of clear, planned focuses on each with a component of challenge that is requesting, however feasible, to see you through the general task. You might have the option to focus on certain undertakings for a more drawn out period, yet for most consideration will be on the melt away after this time. An extreme challenge to be accomplished in an hour is less overwhelming than one that you hope to take two, and you're additionally less inclined to cut yourself any leeway. It's conceivable to shoot away at an errand for this period and accomplish more than you suspected conceivable.

3. The planned component to your objective is significant for a trained way to deal with the activity; however, go for the accomplishment of your objective errand as opposed to adhering unbendingly to the time designation. On the off chance that you accomplish it in under the actual time, that would be preferable – give yourself a congratulatory gesture. If it takes somewhat longer than you suspected, at that point, stay with it to oversee it. Just if you locate that an errand is taking much longer than you foresaw or you hit a total block divider should you reassess your desires. In such a circumstance you may set a lesser objective to be accomplished inside the picked timeframe, or search for a method for moving beyond the impediment that has hindered your advancement, may be looking for an alternate point on the issue or moving to another piece of the general undertaking with the end goal of coming back to the dangerous territory later. Try not to allow a surprising hitch to be a reason for bringing down apparatuses.

4. Toward the finish of each target period, before you enjoy a reprieve, set your next target assignment and make a beginning on it for only a couple of moments. That way, you will come back to work in progress, and the exertion of refocusing will be substantially less.

5. Alright, you can enjoy that reprieve now. Only a couple of moments accomplishing something other than what's expected is commonly enough. It may be a speedy and straightforward upkeep task, an undemanding telephone call, or a chance to extend your legs or loosen up your eyes after a continued spell of PC action. What makes a difference is that it ought to be not the same as the other assignment you have been doing, and you ought not to enable it to form into a protracted redirection. On the off chance that other strengthening undertakings emerge, give them their very own opening on your schedule and return to the primary occupation close by.

Preparing the intensity of the habit

You have a limited measure of vitality every day, and you need to have the option to use it as profitably as could reasonably be expected. In any case, the odds are that a wide range of minor and time-squandering assignments are spending your accessible assets and anticipating you pushing forward those more significant ventures which require supported focus and exertion.

By enrolling the intensity of habit, you can free up the vitality you have to give to the concentrated errands, which will genuinely have any effect on your adequacy. On the off chance that you value carrying a component of imagination to your work and have an intuitive animosity towards anything that bears a resemblance to turning into an animal of habit, support yourself in the information that having a few practices and schedules in your day can give you more vitality to handle the inventive things at different occasions. Consider the plans you experience when you get up in the first part of the day – cleaning your teeth, for instance.

They have gotten imbued – mostly, you start your day. Your considerations are somewhere else while you are doing them – tuning in to the radio or arranging your day – and you don't stress over them. They request no psychological vitality. There are undertakings in your working day, which can be transformed into what might be compared to cleaning your teeth. They may not allow the same incredible degree of mental separation. However, they're undertakings which right now go through pointless vitality. They strive with the various requests upon you for a spot on your bustling calendar – you need to choose when to do them, and stress over them when they are not done.

CHAPTER 6

THE HABITUAL CREATIVITY

"At the point when individuals state to me that they are not imaginative, I expect that they haven't yet realized what is included."

HOW CREATIVE ARE YOU?

How inventive are the individuals you work with? What about your companions? Next time you are at a get-together, ask them. You might be astounded by what they state. I have worked with individuals and organizations everywhere throughout the world. Wherever I go, I locate a similar oddity. Most youngsters believe they're exceptionally innovative; most grown-ups believe they're not. This is a more significant issue than it might appear.

REEXAMINING CREATIVITY

To address these inquiries, it is imperative to be clear about what inventiveness is and how it works practically speaking. There are three related thoughts, which I will intricate as we go on. They are creative minds, which is the way toward inferring things that are absent to our faculties; innovativeness, which is the way toward creating unique thoughts that have worth, and development, which is the way toward placing new ideas into training. There are various confusions about imagination specifically.

"My beginning stage is that everybody has enormous innovative limits as a characteristic aftereffect of being an individual. The test is to create them. A culture of innovativeness needs to include everyone, not only a chosen few."

Uncommon individuals? It is frequently believed that lone exceptional individuals are innovative: that imagination is a unique ability. This thought is fortified by chronicles of inventive symbols like Martha Graham (1894–1991), Pablo Picasso (1881–1973), Albert Einstein (1879–1955), and Thomas Edison (1847–1931). Organizations frequently isolate the workforce into two gatherings: the 'creatives' and the 'suits.' You can ordinarily tell who the creatives are because they don't wear suits. They wear pants, and they come in late because they have been battling with a thought. I don't intend to propose that the creatives are not imaginative. They can be exceptionally original, yet so can anyone if the conditions are correct, including the suits. Everybody has enormous inventive limits. The test is to create them. A culture of imagination needs to include everyone, not only a chosen few.

Different exercises? It is regularly considered exceptional practices, similar to expressions of the human experience, or promoting, or structure, or showcasing. These can be inventive, yet so can anything, including science, arithmetic, educating, working with individuals, drug, running a games group, or a café. Schools, once in a while, have 'imaginative expressions' areas of expertise. I am a firm promoter of a better arrangement for interpretations of the human experience in schools. I will clarify why, later. Be that as it may, imagination isn't restricted to expressions of the human experience. There are numerous explanations behind showing emotions of the human experience in schools, incorporating their job in encouraging imagination, and there are others that are similarly convincing. Simultaneously, different controls, including science and arithmetic, can be equally as innovative as music and move. Inventiveness is conceivable at whatever point we're utilizing our knowledge. In business as well, various organizations are imaginative in multiple regions.

Apple, earth stance, is broadly great at making new items. Others, like Wal-Mart, haven't made any items whatsoever; their zone of advancement is in frameworks, for example, store network the board and evaluating. The espresso chain, Starbucks, is inventive in giving administrations. Starbucks didn't design espresso; it made a specific kind of culture around espresso. As a matter of fact, it invented the $5 mug of espresso, which was somewhat of an achievement, I thought. An advancement in some portion of an association can change its fortunes.

My beginning stage is that everybody has colossal inventive limits as a natural consequence of being an individual. The test is to create them. A culture of innovativeness needs to include everyone, not only a chosen few. Figuring out how to be inventive It's regularly felt that innovative individuals are either brought into the world imaginative or not, similarly as they may have blue or darker eyes, and there isn't a lot of they can do about it. The truth of the matter is, there is a great deal you can do to assist individuals with getting increasingly inventive. They can't peruse or compose, you don't expect that they are not equipped for reading and writing, however, that they haven't been instructed how.

It is the equivalent of innovativeness. At the point when individuals state to me that they are not imaginative, Pundits consider youngsters going crazy and thumping down the furniture instead of continuing ahead with genuine work. Being inventive does typically include toying with thoughts and having a fabulous time, satisfaction, and a creative mind.

Be that as it may, inventiveness is additionally about working in a profoundly centered manner around thoughts and activities, creating them into their best structures and making necessary decisions en route about which work best and why. In each order, imagination additionally draws on ability, information, and control. It's not just about giving up; it's tied in with hanging. For what reason are these issues significant at any rate?

Confronting the upheaval

I mean, this truly not allegorically. There are powers at work now for which there are no points of reference. I realize this is a striking case; however, it legitimized. Human undertakings have consistently been tempestuous. What is particular currently is the rate and size of progress. The two incredible main thrusts are mechanical development and populace development. Together they are changing how we live and work; they are putting an immense strain on the earth's unique assets and changing the idea of governmental issues and culture. New advancements are altering the concept of work all over the place. In the old modern economies, they are enormously diminishing the quantities of individuals in enterprises and callings that were once work concentrated.

New types of work depend progressively on significant levels of expert information, and inventiveness and advancement. The latest innovations specifically require entirely various limits from those needed for the mechanical economy. Assembling is moving to the emanant economies, particularly in Asia and South America, thus also are a considerable lot of the new types of work that rely upon elevated levels of aptitude in structure and data advancements.

Given the speed of progress, governments, and organizations all through the world perceive that instruction and preparing are the keys to the future, and they stress the imperative need to create forces of imagination and development. It is fundamental to develop thoughts for new items and administrations and to keep up a focused edge.

Second, it is significant that instruction and preparing empower individuals to be adaptable and versatile, with the goal that organizations can react to evolving markets.

Third, everybody should conform to a world where, for the vast majority, secure long-lasting work in solitary work is a relic of past times. These mechanical changes, joined with the populace and atmosphere changes, are influencing everybody on earth, and the results are capricious. What is sure is that in the following 50 to 100 years, our kids should defy difficulties that are one of a kind in humanity's history. In the primary segment of the book, I lay out what these powers are and a portion of the difficulties they present.

Reframing our potential

In December 1862, Abraham Lincoln gave his subsequent yearly address to Congress. He was keeping in touch with one month before he marked the Emancipation Proclamation. In his message, he encouraged Congress to see the circumstance they looked with open-minded perspectives. He said this: "The authoritative opinions of the calm past are insufficient to the stormy present. The event is heaped high with trouble. As our case is new, so we should think once again and act over again. We should disenthrall ourselves, and afterward, we will spare our nation."

I love the word: 'disenthrall.' What he implied was that we, as a whole, live our lives guided by thoughts to which we are committed yet which may never again be valid or significant. We are mesmerized or excited by them. To push ahead, we need to shake free of them. Given the difficulties we face now, the most significant move must be by the way we consider our very own capacities and those of our youngsters.

As far as I can tell, many, maybe the vast majority have no clue about their genuine capabilities and gifts. Too many think they have no extraordinary gifts by any stretch of the imagination. My reason is that we came into the world with enormous regular contributions; however, that too hardly any individuals find what they are and significantly less create them appropriately. Amusingly one of the principal explanations behind this enormous misuse of ability is the very procedure that is intended to develop it: training.

Training isn't always a decent word to utilize socially. On the off chance that I am at a gathering and I tell somebody I work in practice, I can here and there observe the blood channel from their face. "Why me?" they're thinking, "Caught with a teacher on my one night out all week." But the off chance that I get some information about their instruction, about their youngsters' tutoring, they stick me to the divider.

They need to discuss their very own encounters. Everybody has solid feelings. Training is one of those points that runs profound with individuals – like religion, legislative issues, and cash. Thus it should. Discipline is indispensable to the achievement of our working lives, to our kids' faces, and long haul worldwide advancement. More than this, it stamps us with an impression of ourselves that is difficult to evacuate.

Probably the best individuals on the planet didn't find real success at school. Regardless of how effective they have become; they frequently convey mystery stress that is not as sharp as they are making out. They incorporate instructors, college educators, corrupt habit chancellors, agents, performers, journalists, specialists, planners, and numerous others. Many succeeded simply after they had recouped from their training.

Numerous individuals adored their time in practice and have done well by it. What of the individuals who didn't? Current ways to deal with instruction and preparing are limped by suspicions about knowledge and innovativeness that have wasted the abilities and smothered the inventive certainty of untold quantities of individuals. This waste stems mostly from a fixation on specific kinds of scholarly capacity and a distraction with state-sanctioned testing — the misuse of ability.

Most teachers have a profound responsibility to helping understudies give a valiant effort. Government officials, as well, give enthusiastic discourses about taking advantage of each understudy's capacities. The misuse of ability may not be purposeful; however, it is fundamental. It is foundational, because state-funded instruction is a framework, and it depends on profound situated suppositions that are never again evident.

Before the center of the nineteenth century, moderately, barely any individuals had any formal instruction. Being instructed was predominantly the benefit of the rare sorts of people who could manage the cost of it. Mass frameworks of government-funded education were grown principally to address the issues of the Industrial Revolution, and, from various perspectives, they reflect the principles of modern creation.

They underline linearity, congruity, and institutionalization. One reason by which the majority are not working is that genuine is natural, versatile, and assorted. A little while before our child began at college in Los Angeles, we came for a direction day. At a certain point, the understudies were removed for a different preparation on program alternatives, and the guardians took to the fund office for a type of pain guiding. We, at that point, had an introduction from one of the educators about our jobs as guardians during our kids' understudy days.

He instructed us to step out concerning their way and extra them a lot of our professional counsel. He gave the case of his child, who had been an understudy at the university a few years prior.

He had initially needed to examine the works of art. The educator and his significant other were not excited at the specific employment prospects that a work of art degree would open up for him. So they were diminished when toward the finish of the first year he said he had chosen to make a significant in something that would be increasingly valuable. They asked their child what he had at the top of the priority list, and he said reasoning. His dad called attention to that none of the massive ways of thinking firms were enlisting at the time.

His child took some way of thinking courses in any case and afterward, in the long run, studied artistry history. After school, he got a new line of work in a global sales management firm. He voyaged, brought home the bacon, and cherished the work and the life.

He landed the position given his insight into old societies, his scholarly preparing in theory, and his adoration for craftsmanship history. Neither he nor his folks could have anticipated that way when he began his school examines. The guideline is the equivalent for everybody.

Life isn't straight. At the point when you pursue your actual north, you make new chances, meet various individuals, have numerous encounters, and make an alternate life. The pecking order of orders in schools depends mostly on suspicions about the organic market in the commercial center.

Industrialized economies left a trail of bombed organizations, seas of obligation, and deep pools of auxiliary joblessness.

Among the most exceedingly awful influenced are youngsters. As I compose this, worldwide degrees of unemployment among youngsters, matured from 15 to 24, is the most noteworthy on record.

In August 2010, the International Labor Organization (ILO) distributed its report on Global Employment Trends for Youth 2010. The report reasons that there are roughly 620 million monetarily dynamic youngsters around the world. Toward the finish of 2009, 81 million of them were jobless, the most noteworthy number ever, and right around 8 million more than in 2007. The adolescent joblessness rate expanded from 11.9 percent in 2007 to 13.0 percent in 2009. The ILO contends that these patterns will have "noteworthy ramifications for youngsters and coming associates of new contestants join the positions of effectively jobless, which is an emergency condition for the youngsters who have dropped out of the work, having lost all expectation of having the option to work for a living." For many youngsters, the future appears to be hopeless and depressed. They have no work and see no possibility of it.

Youth joblessness rates have been touchier to the monetary emergency than grown-up paces of joblessness and, indeed, the recuperation of the activity showcase for youngsters and ladies will, in general, linger behind that of grown-ups. For individuals everything being equal, the monetary recovery, when it comes, won't be simple; and in any event, when it arrives, it won't be anything new.

As Thomas Friedman, creator of the World is Flat, puts it, "The individuals who are trusting that this downturn will end so somebody can again hand them work could have a long pause." Rebuilding the networks that have been left deprived by the downturn will rely upon creative mind, inventiveness, and advancement.

As the ILO report contends, making occupations for the large number of young ladies and men entering the work advertise each year is a primary segment in the way towards wealthier economies. It isn't just the amount yet additionally the nature of employments that issues.

Friedman proceeds, "The individuals who can envision new administrations and new chances and better approaches to select work ... are the new Untouchables. Those with the creative mind to imagine more intelligent approaches to do old employments, vitality sparing approaches to give new administrations, better approaches to pull in old clients or better approaches to join existing advances will flourish."

The arrangement is better instruction and preparing. Here as well, the future can't be the same old thing. "We do not just need a higher level of our children moving on from secondary school and school – more instruction – yet we need a greater amount of them with the correct training. Our schools have a doubly hard assignment, improving perusing, composing, and number juggling yet business enterprise, advancement, and imagination. We're not returning to past times worth remembering without fixing our schools just as our banks."

Samuel J. Parmitano, the Chairman, President, and Chief Executive Officer of IBM, stated, "We possess a world that is associated with different measurements and at a more profound level – a worldwide arrangement of frameworks." It is this remarkable degree of interconnection and interdependency that supports the most significant discoveries in the IBM report.

The examination found that at the highest point of the plans of worldwide business and open division pioneers, there are three broadly shared viewpoints.

In the first place, they accept that a fast heightening of unpredictability is the most significant test standing up to them. They anticipate that it should proceed – undoubtedly to quicken – in the coming years. Second, they are similarly confident that their ventures today are not outfitted to adapt successfully to this unpredictability in the standard condition.

The outcomes of an absence of inventiveness can be severe. Associations that stop are probably going to be cleared aside, and corporate history is covered with the destruction of organizations, and entire businesses, that have been impervious to change. They got stuck in old habits and missed the flood of progress that conveyed increasingly imaginative organizations forward. I once talked at an occasion supper in London to dispatch a rundown of the Fortune Global 500 Companies. The best three organizations were American. Ten years sooner, the best three organizations had all been Japanese.

Presently an expanding number of Chinese organizations are climbing the positions. No association has a guaranteed spot at the highest priority on any rundown. Fortunes rise or fall as per how well they adjust to evolving conditions. One method for depicting the decay of the Japanese organizations is that they were casualties of environmental change. Their general surroundings changed quicker than them, and they endured the results. The economies of China, South America, and India, then again, are adjusting quickly to the new interest for mechanical advancement.

Hardly any individuals would debate that in the eighteenth and nineteenth hundreds of years,

Europe and particularly Great Britain commanded the world socially, politically, and financially. England was the pot of the Industrial Revolution, and its military powers verified the settlements as without a doubt as the English language attacked their societies. At the point when Queen Victoria climbed to the royal position in 1837, she managed the most significant domain ever: the realm on which the sun never set.

If you had gone to her court in 1850 and proposed that this domain would be over inside an age, you would have been giggled out of the structure. But then it was valid. Before the finish of World War, I in 1918, the domain was lethally injured, and, when I was conceived in 1950, it was a memory. Socially, politically, and financially, the twentieth century was overwhelmed by the United States, as doubtlessly as Europe had commanded the nineteenth century. Regardless of whether it will control the 21st century is not yet clear.

As grant-winning US researcher Jared Diamond has appeared, domains will in general breakdown as opposed to blurring away.

Think about the Soviet Union and its fast disintegration during the 1980s and 1990s. All associations are natural and transient. Individuals make them, and they should be continually re-made if they are to endure. At the point when associations come up short, the occupations and networks that rely upon them sway as well. In reality, as we know it where long-lasting work in a similar activity is a relic of days gone by, imagination isn't an extravagance.

It is necessary for individual security and satisfaction. Driving a culture of advancement has radical ramifications for how establishments are composed – regardless of whether they are schools or partnerships – and for styles of authority. Numerous associations put on alternate preparing days to urge their staff to think imaginatively. Yet, like the custom of downpour moving, they frequently belittle the issues they are attempting to understand.

Therefore, this is anything but an ordinary book on inventiveness, offering tips for one week from now's course. It is about the underlying drivers of the issue instead of its side effects. In the last piece of the book, I condense what's associated with handling these more profound issues.

CHAPTER 7

TIME MANAGEMENT

Sorting out your time

Time is not reasonable for most different assets in that it is shared out similarly. We, as a whole, have a similar measure of it every day. The contrasts between us lie by the way we decide to spend it and how far we attempt to extend it. Your point in dealing with your time better is either to decrease the number of hours you spend working or accomplishing more in a similar number of hours. It involves requesting needs. At the point when you state, 'I simply lack time for this,' you are honestly saying, 'Something different is essential to me than this.'

The issue is that, through deficient arranging and checking, we lose control of our calendar and neglect to recognize the significant compensation off and low pay-off requests on our time. We end up saying, 'I haven't timed for this' to a substantial responsibility since we have just spent a lot of it on incidental data. In this section, at that point, we will take a gander at systems for arranging and following the assignments that we have to invest energy. To begin with, in any case, how about we think about how you, as of now, invest your energy.

How you use the time now

It is valuable, before leaving on another arranging system for your time, to give some thoughtfulness regarding how you are right now spending it. Sometimes the executive's programs recommend that you keep up an inflexible time log for two or three weeks. I don't consider this to be vital. However, I do recommend that you do a straightforward observing activity over the time of a few days.

Arranging and following your time

Having inspected how your time presently spent, the subsequent stage is to receive a useful framework for arranging and following your time as the days progressed, many months ahead.

Arranging your time

Viable arranging necessitates that you assess distinctive periods. The overall significance of longer-term and momentary arranging will differ as per the idea of your work; however, you may jump at the chance to take a gander at arranging more than three-time spans. The first, and broadest, maybe a general perspective on the following three months regarding significant destinations. The second, seven days by-week view to be sure that you can fit in the central planning for approaching responsibilities and cutoff times. The third, a nitty-gritty day by day, intend to guarantee that you accomplish a harmony among essential and critical things and undertakings which contribute towards longer-term targets.

Arranging your day an opportunity to design your day isn't before anything else, toward the finish of the past working day. When you start, it will take close to a couple of moments before you pack up for the afternoon. The assignment is finished while your mind is still in work mode and the next morning you are saved any uncertainty and time-squandering while you gear yourself up for

- Choose to what extent you anticipate that exercises should take;
- Choose when you should finish undertakings over the coming days and weeks;

- Recognize what you will require from others all together that you can finish your very own errands.

Following your time

Following is tied in with keeping over the exercises you had arranged – guaranteeing that you are reminded when activities expected, and checking your advancement towards the accomplishment of the goals you have set yourself. The way into this is effortlessness. At every possible opportunity, abstain from recording data in various areas — this issue especially on the off chance that you are utilizing paper-based methods for recording responsibilities. Using a work area journal in the workplace and a pocket journal when you are at gatherings and out and about is a formula for neglected arrangements.

On the off chance that it is fundamental to have data in various organizations, ensure that there is one ace record. Farthest point the measure of the manual movement of data beyond what many would consider possible to evade oversights and limit squandered exertion.

Planning and following instruments

The instruments you use to help planning and following may go from a note pad and journal to a palmtop PC. Pick those that best suit your favored style and the idea of your work. Keep in mind that an inadequately utilized apparatus can hinder instead of upgrade your viability. It might be that your needs are sufficiently served at the underlying finish of the range – a scratch pad to record assignments and general updates, and a journal for arrangements and coordinated duties. Every other instrument is a minor departure from this fundamental design, and expanded modernity doesn't always mean more noteworthy viability. Nonetheless, those of us with enormous quantities of contacts, assignments, and arrangements will need further developed methods for following them.

Paper-based organizers and coordinators

In the 1980s, no self-regarding proficient would be seen without a calfskin bound individual coordinator, and a visit to an office stationery provider today will uncover that while numbers and ranges have declined, there is still bounty around, created in an assortment of styles and costs. The fundamental arrangement is a little ring folio with listed areas containing pre-printed embed pages.

Normal embeds accessible include:

- Year organizers;
- Journals in different arrangements;
- Day by day planning sheets – arrangements and activities;
- Month to month destinations and task planning sheets;
- Phone and address book embeds;
- Pages for notes;
- Spending planning and costs planning.

The thought is that all fundamental working data contained in one advantageous organizer. Clients can switch their consideration effectively from a long haul to a quick view and can quickly refresh data any place they may be. New pages can be embedded and repetitive ones evacuated with the goal that the coordinator remains inconclusively expandable and consistently state-of-the-art.

The drawback is that there might be some need to move data starting with one page, then onto the next, and a portion of the devices, year organizers, for instance, are excessively little for proper use. Likewise, if you have an enormous number of contacts for your location book or need to make a ton of notes, you can discover these segments getting awkward.

What framework is the best for the following time?

Everything relies upon how you like to function. Paper-based frameworks are considerably less ground-breaking as far as to cross-referencing and require a level of duplication. They come up short on the office for programmed updates, and it's simple for things to get lost. Then again, contributing or removing data from PC based frameworks can intrude on the progression of different exercises, and there might be new aptitudes to adapt, for example, the unmistakable letter development required for penmanship acknowledgment. What's more, don't disparage the thingamabob factor. In case you're into devices, it is conceivable to become excited by what your equipment or programming can do, as opposed to what you need it to do.

There is no uncertainty that we are progressively going to innovation to help our association. However, it isn't yet time to announce a conclusion to paper-based techniques. Indeed, even the most mechanically dedicated of us will confess to undertakings where we want to utilize paper – for instance, when mapping out the exercises to be incorporated inside a venture before getting down to point by point planning.

As far as it matters for me, while I utilize the PIM programming on my netbook widely, and synchronize the data it contains with my work area PC and telephone, I will consistently keep a journal to hand, frequently wanting to make a jotted note to be entered later as opposed to interfere with the progression of other movement so as to connect with an electronic gadget.

Planning your time – evaluating time prerequisites

You start the day with, suppose, twelve things on your schedule. What certainty do you have that by the day's end, they will all have been checked off? Not an incredible arrangement except if you have made some gauge of to what extent each assignment is probably going to take, and fitted them in with different duties that make up your day. It isn't just about the certainty and believability support that originates from accomplishing what you set out to do. Assessing the time necessities of assignments enables you to utilize the accessible openings in your day fittingly.

If you have thirty minutes between responsibilities, you need, at every possible opportunity, to fill it with a half-hour task. Finding that an assignment you thought was going to take thirty minutes is genuinely going to take an hour may bring about extra time spent refocusing your consideration when you, in the end, return to it.

You will never accomplish time estimation flawlessness. Assignments will contain unexpected components, and we as a whole tend to overestimate the time taken to finish those undertakings we loathe and to think little of the ones we like. In any case, recessing for a minute to consider what is associated with a company before you pop it into your timetable can enormously help the administration of your working day.

Opening assignments into the day

Your day is probably going to be comprised of fixed duties – arrangements and ordinary planned components – and adaptable ones – the errands on your schedule. Having evaluated the time, you anticipate that these errands should take, you would then be able to get a thought of when you will plan to fit them in. Try not to look to unbendingly design your entire day ahead of time, and don't invest a great deal of energy all the while.

It ought to be a fast and straightforward method for giving your day shape and parity, due assignments into suitable vacancies, not a bureaucratic exercise. Half-hour vacancies are a sensible method for splitting your day, even though for some littler errands, you might need to think as far as quarter-hour spaces. You are gathering a few minor errands – five or six telephone calls, for instance – into a half-hour space. Permit a touch of cushioning in your time gauges for a portion of the inescapable appeals and interferences. There is an extraordinary fulfillment lift to be had from finishing an undertaking in under the time you anticipated that it should take. Yet, you additionally need to keep up your cool when errands are taking longer than arranged. Most importantly, stay adaptable and manage whatever the day tosses at you.

PROCRASTINATION

Some component of delay is both inescapable and vital in a bustling life. However, we give ourselves unnecessary stress and may enormously lessen our adequacy if we enjoy habitual procrastination. It's most likely the most significant time the board issue for a large number of us, and we have to investigate why it happens and what can be done. The first trouble is that we don't admit to ourselves what we are doing. We present ourselves with reasons, for example,

- 'I haven't got all the data I have to handle this activity.'
- 'I don't have time right now to do it equity.'
- 'There are different cutoff times that are all the more squeezing.'
- 'If I do nothing with this, it will likely leave.'

We handle the simpler things and those that might be externally progressively appealing, while the absolute most significant errands

86

stay fixed. Be that as it may, the pressure of not handling a specific chore is regularly more noteworthy than that engaged with completing it. We sit around and vitality agonizing over the things we have not done when with somewhat more settle they could be dispatched to the out-plate. In any case, it isn't merely an issue of guiding ourselves to show more prominent assurance. Procrastination may have become a profoundly instilled work habit that we have supported and reveled throughout the years. The reasons why we delay handling errands might be unpredictable and shifted.

They include:

- Weariness;
- Absence of trust in our capacity to finish the errand;
- The dread of committing an error;
- View of the undertaking as troublesome or upsetting somehow or another;
- Absence of clarity about the prerequisites of the errand or the assets expected to finish it effectively;

Furthermore, putting undertakings off to one more day isn't the main issue. Similarly, as pervasive is the inclination to postpone getting down to the fundamental work close by utilizing minor errands as self-produced preoccupations, we realize what we ought to invest our energy in. We may even be savoring getting our teeth into it, but we experience a challenging obstruction.

We take advantage of any reason to coordinate our consideration somewhere else. Checking email inboxes, getting some espresso, messaging a companion, or dropping in on a most loved web webpage can all of a sudden become significantly more squeezing than the errand we ought to be associated with. We let ourselves know, 'It will just take two or three minutes to do this,' yet once the interference has been made, it leads on to other similarly squeezing little tasks, and thirty minutes is wasted in a matter of seconds.

In our excellent condition, described for what it's worth by promptness of electronic correspondence, courses to interruption are significantly more predominant than they used to be, and the occurrence of procrastination has all the earmarks of being ascending as an outcome. In an ongoing report did by the University of Calgary, it has been noticed that the average self-evaluation score for a propensity towards procrastination has ascended by 39% over the most recent 25 years.

The creator of the examination, Professor Piers Steel, says, 'It's never been more diligently to act naturally trained in all of history than it is currently.' Unfortunately, procrastination is a habit that will, in general, deteriorate the more we humor it. Errands routinely delayed may get challenging to satisfy.

Procedures for beating procrastination

Similarly, as with most issues, acknowledgment of its reality is the initial step to conquering it. Watch out for any inclination to encourage yourself the kind of reasons recorded toward the beginning of this segment. Watch yourself over the coming days and search for any indications of protection from specific assignments. Ask yourself what the reasons are – dread and tension, fatigue, vulnerability, compulsiveness – similar ones won't generally apply.

When you have distinguished the reason(s) it's simpler to choose the most suitable procedures for beating the issue:

Get the agony balance right

The possibility of completing the undertakings you are evading includes a component of saw torment, yet not doing them includes genuine agony. The issue is that while the apparent suffering is imagined as a success – one that deteriorates the more drawn out an errand is deferred – the genuine torment of not doing the undertaking comes as an enduring low-level bothering.

You have to change the harmony between the two, so the agony of not carrying out the responsibility exceeds the apparent torment of doing it. You can accomplish this by – explaining as far as you could tell the outcomes of suspending as now as loss of authority over your life. Presenting punishments for non-execution; – making an open responsibility or opening yourself to be considered answerable for non-culmination of specific assignments. Handle apparent torment by taking note of the recurrence with which errands you have been maintaining a strategic distance from end up being less fearsome than anticipated, and utilize this information as a source of perspective to help conquer future tensions.

Similarly, address the joy side of the condition

What delight do you get from procrastination? The appropriate response, by and large, is none. By what method will you feel if you satisfy the errands you are right now standing up? Envision the finish of seven days where you have accomplished all that you decided to do, and picture what fruition will feel like.

- Ensure that anything making it on to your schedule is a big responsibility and not only an unclear aim. Keep the rundown short, to begin with, and survey what you have accomplished toward the finish of consistently and consistently.

- Don't permit deferred assignments to develop ahead of steam to the point where they become much progressively hard to handle. Orchestrate your schedule, so the jobs you fear most are the ones you manage first. Your reward will be a day or seven days that gets simpler as it comes.

- Schedule explicit occasions in your journal for handling undertakings you don't care for or are standing up.

- Ritualize repetitive repeating undertakings by including them at set times in your timetable until they become installed schedules that request minimal mental vitality. • Tackle weariness by permitting yourself short controlled breaks at foreordained occasions or when a specific extent of an errand has been finished. In any case, keep up your control to guarantee the tears don't turn into an interruption from the primary chore.

- Recognize when the assets available to you are adequate to accomplish a great job. Try not to make progress toward flawlessness.

- Give yourself promptly, encouraging feedback for effectively managing assignments you have been standing up to. It may comprise a psychological congratulatory gesture, a final journal passage, or some essential pleasurable reward.

- Look for a simple purpose of passage to those undertakings where you have been uncertain how to begin. The significant thing is to make a beginning at whatever point.

- Short eruptions of concentrated movement – only 5 or 10 minutes one after another – can function admirably as a method for conquering latency. They serve to defeat the mental obstruction presented by a troublesome or Scheduling your time – assessing time necessities.

You start the day with, suppose, twelve things on your schedule. What certainty do you have that by the day's end, they will all have been checked off? Not an incredible arrangement except if you have made some gauge of to what extent each undertaking is probably going to take, and fitted them in with different duties that make up your day. It isn't just about the certainty and validity help that originates from accomplishing what you see.

Overwhelming task. You can astound yourself by the amount it is conceivable to accomplish in only a couple of moments if you punch openings in an assignment by this implies. All of a sudden, it is never again overwhelming, and you are beginning to accomplish the force expected to convey you towards fulfillment.

Managing unreasonable cutoff times

The best time to check an unreasonable cutoff time is the point at which it is being set. On the chance that you imagine that you are being approached to work to a cutoff time that isn't attainable, show that you have thoroughly considered the timescale as opposed to just dismissing the proposition without a second thought. Receive a positive critical thinking frame of mind.

Set out the phases that should be met to convey on schedule and investigate whether there are any courses through the trouble –, for example, surplus assets that would assist you with meeting the required timescale – or whether it is workable for the cutoff time to be reexamined.

Tragically, cutoff times are rarely set in an ideal working world, and keeping in mind that the timescale for a task may appear to be sensible when seen in disengagement, the odds are that it will cut crosswise over different assignments that likewise have cutoff times.

One strategy you can embrace with the individual setting the cutoff time is to ask them whether it takes need over different cutoff times you are attempting to.

Provided that this is true, which they would wish you to hinder to meet the timescale on the new position. Keep in mind too that the absolute least sensible cutoff times are simply the ones we set. Similarly, as we heap an excessive number of exercises into our day by day schedules, so we overestimate what we will have the option to accomplish in the coming many months.

In certain conditions, there might be cutoff times that are ridiculous yet not exposed to impact. They may emerge from the prerequisites of external bodies, controllers, or customers. Whenever influenced, the central arrangement is to address different requests on your opportunity to free the space that will enable the cutoff time to be met. Indeed, you must do this early enough to have any effect. Before you start work, ensure you are clear what is expected of you, what assets you have available to you, and what extra help you may call upon if essential. The inability to manage these issues is a continuous reason for missed cutoff times.

Planning to comply with your time constraint

Alright, so you have acknowledged the cutoff time. You currently need to design your usage of it. Separate the task or undertaking into a progression of stages, which will lead you to an effective end and attempt to assess the measure of time each will take. Ascertain the number of working days among now and the arranged fulfillment date and ask yourself what you should do every week (or every day if you are managing a short cutoff time) to accomplish it. Work in adequate leeway to consider sudden occasions and postponements, and ensure that, in assessing the time required for each stage, you have assessed different duties which have an approach to your time.

As you move in the direction of fulfillment of your task, utilize the completing point for every one of the phases as an achievement – a time when you can screen your advancement, and guarantee that you are on track. Use them likewise to give yourself the uplifting feedback essential to look after inspiration. Utilize an opportunity to work in some extra adaptability toward the finish of the venture. The cleaning up components are regularly the ones well on the way to be belittled.

Failure to get down to the work

This propensity frequently goes with a lack of common sense. It might be that you don't know you have all the data you need to make a beginning or simply that the completion date appears to be so far off. You persuade yourself that you have full time and will make sure to get down to it in a day or two. Individuals will regularly stall over the beginning of a task since they need trust in their capacity to prevail at it, or they are uncertain where to begin. Whenever influenced by this, at that point, throw away stresses over handling the assignment toward the start and contribute at whatever point has all the earmarks of being the clearest.

The energy you gain from making advances into the task will, as a rule, exceed any wasteful aspects coming about because of stages handled out of request.

Abstain from being let somewhere near others

Frequently, the finish of a venture or task won't be entirely in your grasp, and you will be dependent on the contribution from others if you are to fulfill your time constraint. By and by, significant planning is the way to guaranteeing that others don't present issues for you.

Perceive that they will have needs of their own, which are probably going to contrast from yours. Tell them in a lot of time what it is you require from them and the date by which you will request their info. It by and large sets this date a couple of days before you need it, so any laxity on their part doesn't toss out the calendar for any resulting work you have to do with their information. Make your necessities as clear as could reasonably be expected to evade any error.

Try not to go over the top in looking for flawlessness.

This is another bombing that signs the absence of certainty. It might involve research or data gathering, which is out of extent with the assignment close by and brings about the individual endeavor the undertaking getting hindered and incapable of seeing the wood for the trees.n the other hand, it might be a reluctance to relinquish the pursuit – tenaciously sharpening and cleaning it with the point of creating the ideal employment. You have to stay away from both these inclinations and perceive the time when further exertion doesn't create a proportionate return.

Time the board and ventures

I have alluded to ventures a few times in this section, and it is beneficial putting in no time flat considering the specific requests that tasks place on your time. Concerning this part, we will respect the term 'venture' as including any endeavor prompting an exceptional result, where effective accomplishment requires the fruition of various components over a while. It might be a task you complete altogether without anyone else or may include the contribution of others. One of the significant challenges with venture movement from a period the board viewpoint is that it needs to occur nearby other work.

Beholding back to the breakdown of work by significance and criticalness which we utilized before in this part, it is typically Sector B movement – significant yet not earnest –. It, therefore, might be pushed off the calendar by other, progressively dire weights, which are, in reality, less significant. Care in planning and following your tasks is consequently fundamental. Entire books are composed of venture planning and the board, and there are some mind-boggling systems essential for dealing with ventures with many time-basic errands, conceivably including the contribution of various people or associations.

CHAPTER 8

CAN YOU MANAGE TIME?

We characterize time the board as an individual instead of a social issue in our way of life. It's your concern in case you're worried and excessively occupied. Deal with it on the chance that you can. Make sure to take care of your tabs and appear to deal with time. Be as it may, how about we think on a social level for a minute before we lock into the activity of completely changing you.

As a culture, might we be able to build up a six-hour workday, a thirty-hour work week, and a paid excursion for each specialist? Might we be able to help general elective working game plans, for example, strategic scheduling and occupation sharing? Might we be able to recognize "obsessive worker" as a genuine social issue rather than a symbol of respect? If not, would we say we will check the real value we pay as the general public for human services alongside underemployment and joblessness?

Would you be able to CHANGE?

It's certainly feasible. During the 1950s, we chose to check the danger of a Communist takeover was our most significant need, and we rebuilt society to do it. (A considerable explanation President Eisenhower made the interstate expressway framework, for instance, was as a method for clearing our urban communities in case of an atomic assault.)

Also, in the mid-1960s, John F. Kennedy promised that the nation would have a man on the moon inside the decade, and we did it. Look at how social dispositions have changed toward cigarette smoking over the most recent twenty years. That didn't naturally occur. Individuals endeavored to change those frames of mind.

"Gigantic changes in social mindfulness and qualities are conceivable. In any case, until further notice, chip away at the one piece of society you can change—yourself."

EXACTLY WHAT CAN YOU DO ABOUT THE TIME CRUNCH?

A significant number of us feel that a few or a mind-blowing entirety is crazy. It's typical for such an extent that the inclination has become a way of life, perceived and gained by sponsors. Publicists sell things by associating with buyers' sentiments and adjusting their items and administrations to oblige those ways of life. They aren't stating that we should feel crazy.

They're accepting that we do—and offering a fractional arrangement, a time-saver, an island of peacefulness in a sea of turmoil, one great item that works how it should. It should not shock anyone that the publicizing network is on to us; their examinations, studies, and center gatherings are ceaselessly cutting and dicing our habits and inclinations into littler and increasingly sensible pieces. They know, for instance, that in 2005, there were 126 billion "in a hurry eating events" in the United States. That is more than one for every individual for every day for each man, lady, and kid—a great deal of nibbling.

Invigorated by this information, nourishment makers are anxious to supply the fuel (read: nibble nourishment) that feeds our need to enjoy and helps keep us in a hurry. This accommodation means a $63 billion every year business. The nourishment business, who idealized the drive-through understanding, like this showed us how to eat while driving, a significant performing various tasks ability in this day and age. Most suppliers of merchandise and ventures additionally configuration time-sparing, comfort characteristics into their items, and highlight these attributes in showcasing endeavors.

The PC equipment and programming ventures were based on this reason, and remain as symbols for profitability improvement. However, the longing to oversee time is such an all-inclusive objective, that it keeps on bringing forth simple consideration garments, work sparing machines, electronic toll paths, and open route items for each part of our lives. Our autos can stop themselves; we can pay for somebody to remain in line for us, and can utilize a phone to discover the closest bathroom in a strange city, along these lines improving our lifestyle. A portion of these items serve to isolate us from our condition and take out the requirement for social intercourse—and we feel that these are extra benefits.

Where the woodsman of yesteryear required a trusty blade for managing his condition, we need a pile of apparatuses to set us up right away for work and life and to discover answers to any inquiries we may have promptly. At the point when we're excessively occupied, we purchase out with an item or administration to help get us through physically and mentally. Be that as it may, here once more, we should count the actual cost for such accommodations, in time and cash spent shopping, in expanding reliance, and in the missed delights of cooking and smelling and relishing (and, by and large, biting) nourishment.

We need to check up the toll—on our eyes and stomachs and minds—when we drive ourselves to work ever harder, ever quicker, evermore. At the point when you start keeping track of who's winning right, sometimes you'll additionally begin changing a portion of the choices you make.

Points of confinement to the traditional time management approach

"You can increase additional minutes and even hours consistently by following these tips from the time the executives master," the article in the newspaper paper declares. (You know the sort of writing I'm discussing, the benevolent no one peruses, not to mention purchases, yet that by one way or another flaunts a paid dissemination in the millions.) Among these tips from the master, Lucy Hedrick, creator of 365 Ways to Save time, is:

"If you don't possess energy for perusing, letter-composing, cooking or exercise, rise prior in the first part of the day."

This is, by all accounts, a most loved time-the executives' arrangement. Different specialists, the ones who study rest, gauge that Americans are presently getting sixty to an hour and a half less rest every night than they did ten to fifteen years prior. In addition to the fact that she advises less rest, she likewise figures you ought to.

- "Keep your morning meal quick and straightforward. Attempt a 'blender breakfast' comprising of banana, natural product juice, granola, and a scramble of nectar." And,
- "If your bath needs cleaning, do it during your shower. You can scour as you get done with washing or while your hair conditioner is working."

You could accomplish those things. You could make up a gigantic pitcher of "blender breakfast" and keep it in a cooler in your vehicle so that you could drink it while in transit to work. You could take a waterproof CD player into the shower, so you could tune in to a self-improvement program while you're going at the grout with your toothbrush and flushing the cleanser out of your hair. You could even wear your garments into the shower, similar to the heroin Anne Tyler's epic, The Accidental Tourist, so you could wash your duds while you showered, grouted, and tuned in.

These procedures may work magnificently for certain people. However, others would pay too high a cost for the spared seconds. You may need to bite your morning meal, so you realize you've genuinely eaten; you'll need to live with the burden and a specific section of time while you eat your Grape Nuts. You may need and require the three-minute desert garden of a hot sweltering shower, a bit of morning supernatural occurrence, a delight for body and soul, to begin even the busiest day.

A few, in any case, rise early and practice for forty-five minutes to an hour and a half every morning before biting their way through breakfast and floundering in that hot shower. That works for them. It probably won't work for you. A few of us tune in to music when we run, and others incline toward allowing theirs to minds float.

On the off chance that you were so disposed to benefit as much as possible from your run, you could introduce a speakerphone to your treadmill so you could practice both personality and body at the same time, and appreciate a sublime performing various tasks minute.

Some of you have to force severe requests on your workspace—a spot for everything and everything in its place, with flawless records, a perfect work area, a story you can stroll on. Others are in the fertilizer pile school or work area the executives, and wouldn't fret jumping the heaps of documents and books and periodicals that gather on the floor. I even discovered help for the sloppy work environment. In How to Put More Time in Your Life,

Dru Scott lauds "the mystery joys" of messiness, calling muddled people "dissimilar masterminds" (which, you need to concede, sounds

100

superior to "untidy good-for-nothing"). The fact of the matter is—the exemplary guidelines of time the board doesn't work for everybody. You need to locate your specific manner through the recommendations and activities that you pursue. You will be unable to control a few components of your life, and you may not have any desire to. There are

Bunches of things none of us can control, similar to traffic. On the off chance that you drive a vehicle anyplace more crowded than the outback of Australia, you will stall out in rush hour gridlock. Deal with the progression of traffic? You should attempt to deal with the ebb and flow of the stream in which you swim. If you make an arrangement, someone's going to keep you pausing. A telephone specialist will intrude on your supper. Your manager will dump a very late task on you. Your kid will become ill that day. You need to make that uber introduction before the board. It occurs. The main thing you can do is envision and alter.

CHANGES TO GET CONTROL OF YOUR TIME

You could make enormous scale changes. You could leave your place of employment, leave your family, move to a lodge in the Dakotas, and paint scenes. You could. Be that as it may, you most likely won't and presumably shouldn't. You can roll out small improvements without requiring anyone's assistance or authorization. You can, for instance, figure out how to take four lower than usual breaks a day, or receive any of different tips, as I'll propose in a later section. As you part your way through this book, let yourself investigate the same number of potential outcomes as you can. In any case, by applying your inventiveness, activity, and vitality to this investigation, you will discover approaches to make significant life insisting change.

CHAPTER 9

HOW TO IMPROVE YOUR PRODUCTIVITY?

Efficiency can become down to a single word—FOCUS. There are two kinds of centers you have to ace profitability: First, the capacity to oversee interruptions so you can concentrate minute-to-minute on the job needing to be done. Second, the ability to focus on what's imperative to you in the 10,000-foot view, so you don't squander your day on dumb stuff. We will investigate the two sorts of the center, examine the most recent research regarding the matter, and figure out how to utilize them to ace the aptitudes of concentrating your time on what's most significant and overseeing interruptions when they spring up.

Improve your relational abilities

We don't have business issues. We have individual's issues. At the point when we take care of our skin issues, our business issues are considered settled. Individuals' information is a higher priority than item information. Fruitful individuals construct satisfying and attractive characters, which is the thing that makes them magnetic — this aide in getting agreeable collaboration from others. A pleasing personality is anything but difficult to perceive yet challenging to characterize. It is evident in the manner an individual strolls and talks, his way of speaking, the glow in his conduct, and his complete degree of certainty. A few people never lose their appeal paying little mind to age since it streams both from the face and the heart. A satisfying character is a mix of an individual's disposition, conduct, and articulations. Wearing a lovely coupling is a higher priority than all else you wear. It takes significantly more than a shoeshine and a nail trim to give an individual clean. Enchanting habits used to mask a weak character may work in the short run; however, uncover themselves rather rapidly. Connections dependent on ability and style alone, without character, make life hopeless. Allure without character resembles great looks without goodness.

Be polite to all, yet personal with a couple; dry let those couple of be all around attempted before you give them your certainty. Genuine companionship is a plant of moderate development and must experience and withstand the stuns of misfortune before it is qualified for the label.

LIFE IS AN ECHO

A young man blew up with his mom and yelled at her, "I despise you, I abhor you." Because of the dread of censure, he came up short on the house. He went up to the valley and yelled, "I detest you, I detest you," and back came the vibration, "I loathe you, I abhor you." This was the first time in quite a while life he had heard a reverberation. He got terrified, went to his mom for security, and said there was an awful kid in the valley who yelled: "I abhor you, I despise you." The mother comprehended, and she requested that her child return and shout, "I love you, I love you." The young man proceeded to yell, "I love you, I love you," and back came the reverberation. That showed the young man a thing or two that our life resembles an echo: We get back what we give.

Benjamin Franklin stated, "When you regard others, you are ideal to yourself."

LIFE IS A BOOMERANG

Regardless of whether it is our musings, activities, or conduct, at some point or another, they return and with extraordinary exactness.

Approach individuals with deference on your way up because you will meet them on your way down. The accompanying story is taken from the best. Bits and Pieces. Many years prior, two young men were working their way through Stanford University. Their assets got frantically low, and the thought came to them to draw in Ignacy Paderewski for a piano presentation. They would utilize the assets to help pay their board and educational cost.

The assurance was a ton of cashback then, yet the young men concurred and continued to advance the show. They buckled down, to find that they had netted just $1,600. After the show, the two young men told the incredible craftsman the awful news. They gave him the whole $1,600, alongside a promissory note for $400, clarifying that they would gain the sum at the most punctual conceivable minute and send the cash to him. It resembled the finish of their school vocations. "No, young men," answered Paderewski, "that won't do." Then, tearing the note in two, he restored the cash to them also. "Presently," he let them know, "remove from this $1,600 the entirety of your costs and keep for every one of you 10 percent of the parity for your work. Give me a chance to have the rest." The years go by. World War I went back and forth.

Paderewski, presently head of Poland, was endeavoring to sustain a considerable number of starving individuals in his local land. The primary individual on the planet who could help him was Herbert Hoover, who was responsible for the US Food and Relief Bureau. Hoover reacted, and soon a great many vast amounts of nourishment were sent to Poland. After the destitute individuals were nourished, Paderewski ventured to Paris to express gratitude toward Hoover for the alleviation sent him. "That is good, Mr. Paderewski," was Hoover's answer. "Moreover, you don't recollect it, yet you helped me once when I was an understudy at school, and I was in a difficult situation."

Goodness has a method for returning; that is the idea of the monster. One doesn't need to do great with a craving to get back. It simply happens naturally.

WE SEE THINGS NOT THE WAY THEY ARE BUT THE WAY WE ARE

There is a legend about an insightful man who was sitting outside his town. An explorer came up and solicited him, "What sort of individuals live in this town since I am hoping to move from my present one?" The savvy man asked, "What sort of individuals live where you need to move from?" The man stated, "They are mean, pitiless, impolite." The intelligent man answered, "a similar sort of individuals lives in this town as well." After some time, another voyager stopped by and asked a similar inquiry, and the astute man solicited him, "What sort of individuals live where you need to move from?" And the explorer answered, "The individuals are extremely kind, gracious, amiable, and great." The insightful man stated, "You will locate a similar sort of individuals here as well." What is the lesson of the story? For the most part, we see the world, not how it is but rather how we are. More often than not, other individuals' conduct is a response to our own.

TRUST

I accept all connections are trusted connections, for example, manager worker, parent-child, spouse wife, understudy/instructor, purchaser/vendor, client/sales rep. How might we have trust without trustworthiness? Emergency in confidence indeed implies crisis in truth. Trust comes about because of being reliable. What are the elements that fabricate faith?

- Reliability - gives consistency and originates from duty.
- Consistency - constructs certainty.

- Respect- - to self as well as other people gives nobility and shows a minding mentality.

- Fairness- - requests to equity and uprightness.

- Openness- - shows two-way traffic.

- Congruence- - activity and words fit. On the off chance that an individual says a certain something and acts in an unexpected way, how might you believe that individual?

- Competence- - comes when an individual has the capacity and the demeanor to serve.

- Integrity- - the key fixing to trust.

- Acceptance notwithstanding our push to improve we have to acknowledge each other with our pluses and minuses.

- Character- - an individual may have all the skill however on the off chance that he needs character he can't be trusted.

Trust is a more noteworthy compliment than affection. There are a few people we love however we can't confide in them. Connections resemble financial balances: The more we store, the more noteworthy they become, in this way, the more we can draw from them. Be that as it may, in the event that you attempt to draw without storing, it prompts frustration. Ordinarily we believe we are overdrawn however as a general rule we might be under kept. The following are a portion of the outcomes of poor connections and the absence of trust.

What are Some Factors That Prevent Building and Maintaining Positive Relationships?

The greater part of them are clear as crystal or expounded on later in this section.

- Selfishness
- Lack of politeness

- Inconsiderate conduct
- Not meeting responsibilities
- Rude conduct
- Lack of trustworthiness and genuineness
- Self-centeredness - individual all enveloped with himself makes a truly little bundle.
- Arrogance - An egotistical individual is content with his assessment and information. That will promise him unending obliviousness.
- Conceit - Since nature hates a vacuum, she fills void heads with vanity.

THE DIFFERENCE BETWEEN EGO AND PRIDE

The greatest obstacle in building a positive relationship is Ego. Personality is self-inebriating. Self-image is negative pride bringing about egotism. Solid pride is an inclination of the joy of achievement with quietude. Self-image gives a swollen head while pride gives a swollen heart.

A major head gives a major migraine though a major heart gives quietude. Regardless of what the size of an individual's achievements is, there will never be a reason for having a major head. Pride, yes; enormous head, no.

To an egocentric individual, the world starts, closes and rotates around him. An egomaniac can be entertaining as a matter of course. A manager solicited one from his representatives how seriously he needed a raise. The representative stated, "Genuine gravely. I have been appealing to God for one." The manager answered, "You won't get it since you passed me by." An egomaniac talks and looks down on others.

WHAT IS THE DIFFERENCE BETWEEN SELFISHNESS AND SELF- - INTEREST?

It is critical to comprehend the qualification between these two words. Self-centeredness is negative and damaging. It decimates connections since it depends on negative qualities. It has confidence in the success/lose standard. Personal responsibility is sure. It invites success, genuine feelings of serenity, great wellbeing and joy. Personal circumstance puts stock in win/win. Jealousy/Jealousy- - Crab Mentality

What is crab mindset? Do you know how they get crabs? They put a case with one side open for the crabs to stroll in. It has a base yet no top. At the point when the case is full, they close the fourth side. The crabs could without much of a stretch creep out of the crate and go free. Yet, this doesn't occur, on the grounds that the crab attitude doesn't allow it to occur.

The minute one crab fires slithering up, the others pull it down and no one gets out. Think about where they all end up? They all get cooked. Something very similar is valid with individuals who are envious. They never excel throughout everyday life and keep others from succeeding. Envy is an indication of poor confidence. It is an all-inclusive characteristic. The greatest test comes when envy turns into a national character. Nations start declining, bringing about tragic ramifications for coming ages. Envy debases individuals.

"One Should Have an Open Mind Rather Than an Empty Mind"

What is the distinction between a receptive outlook and an unfilled personality? A receptive outlook is adaptable; it assesses and may acknowledge or dismiss thoughts and ideas dependent on merit. An unfilled personality is a dumping ground for good and terrible. It acknowledges without assessment.

STEPS TO BUILDING A POSITIVE PERSONALITY

Stage 1: Accept Responsibility

At the point when individuals acknowledge extra duty they are really giving themselves an advancement. Capable conduct is to acknowledge responsibility and that speaks to development. Acknowledgment of obligation is an impression of our mentality and nature we work in. A great many people rush to assume praise for what goes right however not very many would acknowledge obligation when things turn out badly. An individual who doesn't acknowledge duty isn't vindicated from being capable. Our goal is to develop mindful conduct. Dependable conduct ought to be instilled directly from youth. It can't be educated without a specific level of submission.

Individuals who don't acknowledge duty move the fault to their folks, instructors, qualities, God, destiny, karma, or the stars. Johnny stated, "Mother, Jimmy broke the window." Mama asked, "How could he do it?" Johnny answered, "I tossed a stone at him, and he dodged." People who utilize their benefits without tolerating obligation, as a rule, wind up losing them. Commitment includes attentive activity.

Triviality Causes Us to Ignore Our Responsibilities

Consider it. Unimportant personalities are caught up with passing the buck instead of doing what should be finished.

Social Responsibility

Antiquated Indian insight instructs us that our first obligation is to the network, second to our family, and third to ourselves — a general public beginning declining when this request is turned around. Social duty should be the ethical commitment of each resident. Obligation and opportunity go connected at the hip. A productive member of society indicates that he is eager to pull his weight.

Social orders are not obliterated by the exercises of scalawags yet by the latency of competent individuals. What a Catch 22! On the off chance that they can endure decimation by being latent, how might they be great? The inquiry, would they say they are releasing their social obligation?

For wickedness to prosper, great individuals need to sit idle, and underhandedness will thrive. - Edmund Burke

Stage 2: Consideration

At some point, a ten-year-old kid went to a frozen yogurt shop, sat at a table, and asked the server, "What amount is a gelato?" She stated, "seventy-five pennies." The kid began including the coins he had in his grasp. At that point, he solicited how much a little cup from frozen yogurt was. The server restlessly answered, "sixty-five pennies." The kid stated, "I will have the little dessert cup." He had his frozen yogurt, took care of the tab, and left. At the point when the server came to get the empty plate, she was contacted. Underneath were ten one-cent coins as a tip. The young man had thought for the server before he requested his ice-cream. He indicated affectability and mind. He thought of others before himself.

On the off chance that we as a whole suspected like the young man, we would have an incredible spot to live. Show thought, civility, and pleasantness. Astuteness shows a minding frame of mind.

Stage 3: Think Win/Win

A man kicked the bucket, and St. Dwindle inquired as to whether he might want to go to paradise or damnation. The man asked as to whether he could see both before choosing. St. Diminish took him to hellfire first, and the man saw a major lobby with a long table, bunches of nourishment on it, and music playing. He likewise observed columns of individuals with pale, tragic appearances. They looked starved, and there was no giggling.

Furthermore, he watched one more thing. Their options were limited to four-foot forks and blades, and they were attempting to get the nourishment from the focal point of the table to place into their mouths. Be that as it may, they proved unable. At that point, he went to see paradise. There he saw a significant lobby with a long table, with loads of nourishment on the table and music playing.

He saw lines of individuals on the two sides of the table with their options limited to four-foot forks and blades too. In any case, he saw there was something other than what's expected here. Individuals were giggling and were well-nourished and sound looking. He saw that they were nourishing each other over the table. The outcome was joy, flourishing, happiness, and delight since they were not considering themselves alone; they were thinking win/win. The equivalent is valid for our lives. At the point when we serve our clients, our families, our managers, and representatives, we naturally win.

Stage 4: Choose Your Words Carefully

An individual who says what he enjoys, for the most part, winds up hearing what he doesn't care for. Be prudent. Affability comprises of picking one's words cautiously and knowing how far to go. It likewise implies comprehending what to state and what to leave inferred.

Ability without propriety may not generally be attractive. Words reflect demeanor. Words can and annihilate connections. An ill-advised selection of words has harmed more individuals than by any catastrophic event. Pick what you state as opposed to state what you pick.

That is the distinction between intelligence and stupidity. Inordinate talking doesn't mean correspondence. Talk less; state more. A trick talk without deduction; an intelligent man thinks before talking. Words that stood up of harshness can cause hopeless harm. How guardians address their youngsters in numerous cases shapes their kids' fate.

EXPRESSED WORDS CAN'T BE RETRIEVED

A rancher defamed his neighbor. Understanding his error, he went to the evangelist to request absolution. The evangelist guided him to take a pack of quills and drop them in the focal point of the town. The rancher did as he was told. At that point, the evangelist requested that he proceed to gather the quills and set them back taken care of. The rancher attempted, however, couldn't as the feathers had all overwhelmed. At the point when he came back with the vacant pack, the minister stated, "something very similar is valid about your words.

You dropped them rather effectively; however, you can't recover them, so be extremely cautious in picking your words."

Stage 5: Don't Criticize and Complain

At the point when I discuss analysis, I allude to the negative reviews. For what reason would it be a good idea for us not to scrutinize? At the point when an individual is examined, he gets guarded. Does that mean we ought to never scrutinize, or would we be able to give positive analysis? A pundit resembles a busybody who makes the driver distracted.

Positive Criticism

What is a useful analysis? Censure with a soul of support as opposed to as a putdown. Offer arrangements in your review. Condemn the behavior, not the individual, since when we scrutinize the individual, we hurt their confidence. The privilege to examine accompanies the longing to help. For whatever length of time that the demonstration of scrutinizing doesn't offer delight to the provider, it is alright. When giving analysis turns into a joy, the time has come to a stop. A few proposals for providing a review that propels others:

- Be a mentor - scrutinize with a supportive frame of mind. A mentor reprimands to help improve the execution of the competitor.
- Understanding and concern will go about as an inspiration.
- The mentality ought to be remedial as opposed to jail.
- Be explicit, instead of making statements like "you generally" or "you never." Vague analysis causes hatred.
- Get your realities right. Try not to form a hasty opinion. We as a whole reserve the privilege to our suppositions, yet we don't reserve the option to mistaken certainties. Try not to hurry to condemn.
- Maintain your cool yet be firm.
- Criticize to convince, not threaten.
- If the analysis is given correctly, it will decrease the requirement for reiteration.
- Criticize in private, not out in the open. Why? Since it keeps up altruism while extensive analysis can be mortifying.

- Give the other individual a chance to clarify his side.
- Show them how they would profit by amending their mix-up.
- Criticize the presentation, not the entertainer. Try not to express close to home hatred.
- Call attention to the misfortune emerging from the activity and the antagonistic results of not revising it.
- Ask for recommendations for development.
- Question the activity, not the purpose. If the aim is being referred to, at that point, it is smarter to end the relationship.
- Keep analysis in context. Try not to try too hard. Analysis resembles giving the drug. The medicine ought to be the correct blend with an ideal dose. An excess of will has antagonistic impacts and excessively little Willie insufficient. So also, analysis ought to be kept in context. Given in a definite route in the correct dose, it can do some amazing things.
- If individuals who are being scrutinized acknowledge their misstep and concoct positive recommendations, salute them.
- Close on a positive note with appreciation.

Getting Criticism

There might be times when we are condemned, evenhandedly, or illegally. The best individuals on the planet have been criticized. Supported analysis can be instrumental and ought to be taken decidedly as criticism. Unjustified review truly is a compliment in a mask. Normal individuals detest victors. At the point when individuals are not fruitful, pundits have nothing to discuss. The primary way you will never be scrutinized is if you don't do anything, say nothing or have nothing. You will wind up being a significant nothing. Out of line analysis originates from two sources:

1. Obliviousness. At the point when analysis leaves numbness, it can without much of a stretch be wiped out or revised by bringing mindfulness.
2. Envy. At the point when analysis leaves desire, accept it as a compliment.

In camouflage. You are by and large unreasonably condemned because the other individual needs to be the place you are. The tree that bears the most natural products additionally gets the most stones.

Powerlessness to acknowledge valuable analysis is a sign of weak confidence.

Recommendations for tolerating analysis:

Take it in the correct soul. Acknowledge it generous instead of hesitantly. Gain from it. Acknowledge it with a receptive outlook, assess it, and on the off chance that it bodes well, actualize it. Be grateful to the individual who gives a useful analysis since he has good intentions and has helped you. An individual with high confidence acknowledges the positive review and turns out to be better, not severe.

The issue with a great many people is they would prefer to be commended and lose than be scrutinized and win.

Grumblings

A few people are constant grumblers. If it is hot, it is excessively hot. On the off chance that it is cold, it is too cold. Consistently is an awful day. They grumble regardless of whether everything goes right. For what reason is it not a smart thought to gripe? Since half of the individuals couldn't care less on the off chance that you have an issue and the other half are upbeat that you have a point. What is the purpose of whining? Nothing leaves it. It turns into a character characteristic. Does that mean we ought to never gripe or welcome protests? Not under any condition. Much the same as analysis, if it is done positively, grievances can be valuable.

A helpful rally:

a. shows that the grumbler cares.
b. gives the beneficiary of objections another opportunity to address himself.

Stage 7: Put Positive Interpretation of Other People's Behavior

Without adequate realities, individuals intuitively put a negative understanding of others' activities or inactions. Few people experience the ill effects of "suspicion"; they think the world is out to get them. That isn't valid. By beginning a constructive note, we have a superior possibility of building a satisfying character bringing about great connections. For instance, how regularly have we put through a call and not get an answer from the other party for two days, and the first idea that rings a bell is, "They never minded to restore my call" or "They disregarded me." That is negative.

Possibly:

- They attempted, yet couldn't traverse
- They left the message we didn't get
- They had a crisis
- They never got the message

There could be numerous reasons. It merits giving the advantage of the uncertainty to the next individual and beginning a positive note.

Stage 8: Be a Good Listener

Ask yourself these inquiries. How can it make you feel when you needed someone to hear you out?

- Did they accomplish more talking than tuning in?
- They couldn't help contradicting the principal thing you said.
- They interfered with you at each progression.
- They were fretful and finished each sentence you began.
- They were physically present yet rationally missing.
- They heard, however, didn't tune in. You needed to rehash something very similar multiple times because the other individual wasn't tuning in.
- They reached resolutions inconsequential to certainties.
- They posed inquiries on disconnected points.
- hey were nervous and diverted.
- They were not tuning in or focusing.

Every one of these things shows a lack of engagement in the individual or the theme and a complete absence of obligingness.

There could be scholarly boundaries, for example, language, understanding, and so on. To move others to talk, be a decent audience. Listening shows minding. At the point when you show a minding demeanor toward someone else, that individual feels significant. When he feels significant, what occurs? He is increasingly persuaded and progressively responsive to your thoughts.

Stage 9: Discuss but Don't Argue

There are a few characters that can be marked as contentious, and that shows in their behavior and connections. Contentions can be kept away from and a great deal of grief forestalled by being somewhat cautious. The ideal approach to win a dispute is to stay away from it. A claim is one thing you will always lose. On the chance that you win, you lose; on the off chance that you lose, you lose. On the off chance that you earn a contention, however, lose a great job, client, companion, or marriage, what sort of triumph is it? Vacant. Disputes are resulting from the swelled self-image. Contending resembles taking on a losing conflict. Regardless of whether one wins, the expense might be more than the triumph is value. Enthusiastic fights leave a remaining hostility irrespective of whether you win. In contention, the two individuals are attempting to have the final word. The dispute is simply a clash of inner selves and results in a hollering challenge. A more magnificent trick than the person who knows everything is the person who contends with him.

Is It justified, despite all the trouble?

The more contentions you win; the fewer companions you have. Regardless of whether you are correct, is it worth contending? The appropriate response is quite self-evident. A major no. Does that mean one ought to never raise a point? One should, however delicately and carefully by saying something nonpartisan, for example, "given my data . . ." If the other individual is factious, regardless of whether you can refute him, is it justified, despite all the trouble? I don't think so. Do you come to your meaningful conclusion a subsequent time? I wouldn't. Why? Since the contention is originating from a shut personality attempting to demonstrate who is correct instead of what is right. For instance, at a social party, particularly after a couple of beverages, somebody may state definitively, "The present year's fare figures are $50 billion."

You happen to realize that his data is mistaken, and the correct figure is $45 billion. You read it in the paper that morning, or you heard it on the radio while in transit to the social affair, and you have a release in your vehicle to substantiate it. Do you come to your meaningful conclusion? By saying, "My data is that the fare figure is $45 billion." The other individual responds, "You don't have the foggiest idea what you are discussing.

I know precisely what it is, and it is $50 billion." At this point, you have a few options:

1. Come to your meaningful conclusion again and start a contention.
2. Run and bring the notice from your vehicle and ensure you refute him.
3. Maintain a strategic distance from it.
4. In the event that one needs to achieve extraordinary things in life one needs to rehearse development. Development implies not getting ensnared in immaterial things and negligible contentions.

What is the Difference Between an Argument and a Discussion?

a. A contention tosses heat; an exchange tosses light.
b. One stems from sense of self and a shut personality while different originates from a receptive outlook.
c. A contention is a trade of numbness though a dialog is a trade of information.
d. A contention is an outflow of temper though a dialog is a declaration of rationale.
e. A contention attempts to demonstrate who is correct though a dialog attempts to demonstrate what is correct.

It isn't beneficial to dissuade a biased personality; it wasn't contemplated into him so you can't reason it out. A bias and a major mouth for the most part lead to intriguing however silly contentions. So as to examine, let the other individual express his side of the case without interference. Give him a chance to blow steam. Try not to attempt to refute him on each point. Never let him drag you to his level. Treat him with cordiality and regard; that will confound him. Despite the reason, the most ideal approach to diffuse the circumstance is to:

Be Grateful but Do Not Expect Gratitude

Appreciation is a delightful word. We should be grateful. Appreciation is an inclination. It improves our character and manufactures character. Appreciation creates out of quietude. It is an inclination of gratefulness toward others. It is passed on through our demeanor towards others and reflects in our behavior. Appreciation doesn't mean responding great deeds since appreciation isn't give and take. A decent deed can't be dropped by a check. Things, for example, benevolence, comprehension, and tolerance can't be reimbursed. What does appreciation educate us? It truly shows us the specialty of participation and comprehension. Appreciation must be earnest.

A basic thank-you can be benevolent. Commonly we neglect to be appreciative to the individuals nearest to us, for example, our mate, our family members, our companions. Appreciation would rank among the top characteristics that structure the character and character of a person with respectability. Personality holds up traffic of demonstrating appreciation.

A charitable frame of mind changes our standpoint throughout everyday life. With appreciation and quietude, right activities fall into place. Appreciation should be a lifestyle, something which we can't give enough of. It can mean a grin, or a thank you, or a signal of appreciation.

Think about your most valuable belongings. What makes them unique? Much of the time, the blessing is less noteworthy than the provider. Rarely are we appreciative for the things we as of now have. Recollect and attempt to review the individuals who affected your life. Your folks, educators, any individual who invested additional energy to support you. Maybe apparently they simply carried out their responsibility. Not so much. T

hey eagerly yielded their time, exertion, cash and numerous different things for you. They did it because of affection and not for your appreciation. Sooner or later, an individual understands the exertion that went in to assist them with molding their future. Maybe it isn't past the point where it is possible to say thanks to them. What's more, the time has come to respond. Love requires penance.

Avoid Bearing Grudges. Forgive and never look back

Try not to be a city worker. Have you heard the expression I can excuse however I can't overlook? At the point when an individual will not excuse, he is locking entryways that some time or another he may need to open. When we hold feelings of spite and harbor hatred, who are we harming the most? Ourselves.

Jim and Jerry were cherished companions however for whatever reasons, the relationship self-destructed and they hadn't represented 25 years. Jerry was on his deathbed and would not like to enter endlessness with crushing sadness. So he called Jim, apologized and stated, "How about we excuse one another and be accomplished for the past." Jim thought it was a smart thought and chosen to visit Jerry at the medical clinic. They made up for lost time with 25 years, fixed up their disparities and put in several hours together. As Jim was leaving, Jerry yelled from behind, "Jim, just in the event that I don't bite the dust; recollect, this absolution doesn't tally."

Life is too short to even consider holding feelings of spite. It isn't justified, despite any potential benefits.

A POUND OF BUTTER

There was a rancher who offered a pound of spread to the bread cook. One day the cook chose to gauge the spread to check whether he was getting a pound and he found that he was most certainly not. This incensed him and he prosecuted the rancher. The judge inquired as to whether he was utilizing any measure. The rancher answered, love Honor, I am crude. I don't have a legitimate measure, yet I do have a scale." The judge asked, "At that point how would you gauge the margarine?"

The rancher answered "Your Honor, well before the dough puncher began purchasing spread from me, I have been purchasing a pound portion of bread from him. Consistently when the pastry specialist brings the bread, I put it on the scale and give him a similar load in margarine. On the off chance that anybody is to be accused, it is the bread cook." What is the lesson of the story? We get back in life what we provide for other people.

At whatever point you make a move, pose yourself this inquiry: Am I giving reasonable incentive for the wages or cash I want to make? Genuineness and contemptibility become a habit. A few people practice untrustworthiness and can lie with a straight face. Others lie so a lot of that they don't have the foggiest idea what the fact of the matter is any longer. Yet, who are they misleading? Themselves - more than any other person. Genuineness can be put crosswise over tenderly. A few people invest heavily in being mercilessly legit.

It appears they are getting a greater kick out of the severity than the trustworthiness. Selection of words and respect are significant.

Truth May Not Always Be What You Want to Hear

One can be honest without being coldblooded yet that may not generally be the situation. The most significant obligation of a fair companion is to be honest. A few people, so as to abstain from going up against agonizing certainties, select companions who disclose to them what they need to hear. They kid themselves regardless of the way that where it counts they realize they are not being honest. Genuine analysis can be agonizing.

On the off chance that you have numerous colleagues and scarcely any companions, the time has come to step back and investigate the profundity of your connections. An absence of trustworthiness is some of the time marked as politeness, advertising or legislative issues. Be that as it may, is it actually so? The issue with lying is that one needs to recollect one's falsehoods.

- Harmless exaggerations?
- Sweet talk?

BE CAREFUL WITH HALF-TRUTHS OR MISREPRESENTATION OF TRUTHS

There was a mariner who dealt with a similar vessel for a long time. One night he got an alcoholic. This was the first occasion when it at any point occurred. The chief recorded it in the log, "The mariner was tanked today around evening time." The mariner read it, and he realized this remark would influence his profession, so he went to the skipper, apologized, and requested that the commander include that it just happened once in three years, which was the finished truth. The commander won't and stated, "What I have written in the log is a reality." The following day it was the mariner's go to fill in the log. He expressed, "The commander was calm today around evening time."

The skipper read the remark and requested that the mariner change or add to it clarifying the total truth since this inferred the chief was flushed each other night. The mariner told the skipper that what he had written in the log was a reality.

Be Sincere

Truthfulness involves plans and challenging to demonstrate. We can accomplish our objectives by wanting to help other people.

Avoid Pretense

Asking a companion in a tough situation, "Is there anything I can accomplish for you," is genuinely irritating. It is a higher amount of eyewash and misrepresentation. On the off chance that you genuinely need to help, consider something fitting to be done and afterward do it.

Numerous individuals put on the shroud of genuineness more out of childishness than substance, trusting that some time or another, they could guarantee the privilege to get help. Avoid foolish and fake merriments. Alert - Sincerity is no proportion of decision-making ability. Somebody could be earnest yet off-base.

Practice Humility

Certainty without quietude is presumption. Lowliness is the establishment of everything being equal. It is an indication of significance. Complete quietude draws in, yet false modesty reduces.

Numerous years prior, a rider ran over individual warriors who were attempting to move a substantial log without progress. The corporal was holding on as the men battled. The passenger asked the corporal for what good reason he wasn't making a difference.

The corporal answered, "I am the corporal; I give arranges." The rider got off, went up, and remained by the warriors, and as they were lifting the log, he helped them. With his assistance, the record got moved.

The rider discreetly mounted his steed and went to the corporal and stated, "whenever your men need assistance, send for the Commander-in-Chief." Then, the corporal and his men discovered that the rider was George Washington.

The message is entirely clear. Achievement and modesty go connected at the hip. At the point when others blow your horn, the sound goes further. Consider it? Effortlessness and quietude are two signs of significance.

Modesty doesn't mean self-belittling behavior. That would add up to putting down oneself.

Be Understanding and Caring

Seeing someone we as a whole commit errors and here and there, we are heartless toward the necessities of others, particularly those very near us. This prompts frustration and disdain. The response to dealing with disappointment is understanding. Connections don't come about because individuals are impeccable. They come about as a result of comprehension. There is more delight in being a minding individual than in simply being a decent individual.

A minding frame of mind fabricates generosity, which is the best sort of protection that an individual can have, and it doesn't cost a thing. A few people substitute cash for minding and comprehension. Being understanding is unquestionably more significant than money, and the ideal approach to be comprehended is to get it. What's more, the premise of genuine correspondence is additionally to get it.

Practice Generosity

It is an indication of enthusiastic development. Being liberal is being astute and kind without being inquired. Open-minded individuals experience the lavishness of life, which a narrow-minded individual can't dream of. Be circumspect; narrow-mindedness brings its retribution. Be touchy to other individuals' sentiments.

Be Tactful

Judgment is significant in any relationship. Class is the capacity to make a point without distancing the other individual.

Thoughtfulness

Cash will purchase an incredible canine, yet just consideration will make him sway his tail. It is never too early for thoughtfulness since we don't have the foggiest idea how before long is past the point of no return. Benevolence is a language the hard of hearing can hear

What's more, the visually impaired can see. It is smarter to treat a companion with thoughtfulness while he is living than show blooms on his grave when he is dead. A demonstration of graciousness makes a distinct vibe great paying little respect to whether he is doing it or it is done to him. Kind words never hurt the tongue.

Practice Courtesy daily

Affability is thought for other people. It opens entryways that would not generally open. A considerate individual who isn't sharp will go further in life than an impolite, however keen individual. It is the apparently insignificant details that have a significant effect. Have you, at any point, been nibbled by an elephant? The most obvious answer is no. Do you, at any point, been bitten by a mosquito? The majority of us have. It is the little aggravations that test tolerance. Politeness is made of merely numerous unimportant penances. Little cordialities will take an individual a lot more remote than keenness. Culture is a branch of profound good behavior. It costs only pays well. Nobody is too enormous or too occupied to even think about practicing kindness. Obligingness implies giving your seat to the old or the incapacitated. Graciousness can be a comforting grin; bless your heart. It is a little speculation, yet the adjustments are huge. It upgrades the other individual's self-esteem. Obligingness requires lowliness. It is appalling when individuals become repulsive because they bring down their positive characteristics. I have caught individuals saying with satisfaction, "I can be quite unpleasant." Scatter the seeds of graciousness in any place you can. Some will undoubtedly flourish and raise you according to other people.

CHAPTER 10

THE HEALING POWER OF HUMOR

Dr. Norman Cousins, the creator of Anatomy of an Illness, is a prime case of how an individual can fix himself of a terminal ailment. He had a 1-in-500 possibility of recuperation. However, Cousin needed to demonstrate that if there were in any way similar to mind over the issue, he'd make it a reality. He assumed if negative feelings caused harmful synthetic compounds in our body, at that point, the turnaround must be genuine as well. Positive emotions, similar to bliss and giggling, would bring positive synthetic compounds into our framework.

He moved from the emergency clinic to lodging and leased funny motion pictures and truly relieved himself by giggling. Therapeutic assistance is significant. However, the will to live for the patient is similarly, if not increasingly substantial. A funny bone could be a lifeline. Also, it makes life's misfortunes simpler to deal with.

Don't Be Sarcastic and Put Others Down

Antagonistic individuals' amusingness may incorporate mockery, putdowns, and negative comments.

Any funniness, including parody that ridicules others, is in poor taste. Damage is excused more effectively than an insult.

At the point when somebody reddens with humiliation when somebody diverts a hurt, when something consecrated is made to seem reasonable when somebody's shortcoming gives the giggling when obscenity is required to make it bright. When a youngster is brought to tears or when everybody can't participate in the chuckling, it's a sick joke.

To a perverted person, everything is exciting, since it is transpiring else. It's anything and also an exceptional sight to see young men tossing stones at frogs to have a fabulous time. The young men's fun methods demise to the frogs. It isn't a good time for the frogs. Cleverness can be significant or hazardous, contingent upon whether you are snickering with somebody or at somebody. At the point when diversion includes ridiculing or disparaging others, it isn't in great taste, nor is it honest. Offending others can be remorseless. A few people get

Their enjoyment by putting others down. Mockery distances individuals. It is a smart thought to keep humor generally safe.

To Have a Friend, Be a Friend

We continue searching for the correct boss, the right representative, life partner, parent, kid, etc. We overlook that we must be the ideal individual, as well. Experience has indicated that there is no perfect individual, no excellent activity, no ideal life partner. At the point when we search for flawlessness, we are disillusioned because all we find is that we exchanged a lot of issues for another arrangement of items. Having lived in the

West for more than 20 years, I have seen that with the high separation rate, how it is, individuals find after they get hitched for the second time that their new mate doesn't have the issues of the first yet has a new arrangement of items. So also, individuals change occupations or fire representatives searching for the correct one to find that they exchanged a lot of issues for another. We should attempt to work around these difficulties and make separating or terminating the last instead of the main retreat.

Penance

Kinship takes penance. Building companionships and connections take punishment, dedication, and development. Penance removes going from one's way and never occurs coincidentally. Childishness pulverizes kinships. Easygoing associates come simple yet obvious companionships set aside some effort to fabricate and exertion to keep. Companionships are put to tests, and when they suffer, they become more grounded.

We should figure out how to perceive fake connections. Genuine companions would prefer not to see their companions hurt. Genetic kinship gives more than it gets and remains by misfortune.

Faint-hearted ally

A faint-hearted ally resembles a financier who loans you his umbrella when the sun is sparkling and takes it back the moment it downpours. Two men were going through the woods and went over a bear. One of them immediately climbed a tree, yet the other was not able, so he lay on the ground and played dead.

The bear sniffed around his ear and left. The individual from the tree descended and asked him, "What did the bear let you know?" The man answered, "He stated, don't confide in a companion who betrays you in peril." The message is as dear as light. Shared trust and certainty are the establishment stone of all fellowships.

Fellowships can be classified as pursues:

1. Award of joy. You are a companion insofar as the relationship is engaging and fun, i.e., a fickle companion.
2. Kinship of comfort. This is the place individuals make companionships to pick up favors. These fellowships last until the

helpfulness of the other individual finishes. These fellowships are not changeless.

3. True kinship. This depends on shared regard and profound respect. Genuine companions are individuals who have the benefit of one another on a fundamental level and act as needs are. Great deeds return to us as great companions. There is enduring goodness on the two sides. It depends on character and duty.

Flourishing brings companions, affliction uncovers them. Reasonable climate kinship is portrayed well by the accompanying sonnet: Rejoice, and men will look for you; Upset, and they turn and go; They need a full proportion of all your pleasure, But they needn't bother with your hardship. Be happy, and your companions are many; Be dismal, and you lose them all. There are none to decrease your nectared wine, But alone you should drink life's nerve.

Individuals who are genuine companions in the real sense help each other, yet these are not favors. They are acts accidental to fellowship. What's more, if they don't help, they would bomb in their connections. Connections don't only occur; they set aside some effort to fabricate. They are based on thoughtfulness, comprehension, and selflessness, not on desire, narrow-mindedness, puffed up inner selves, and inconsiderate behavior.

Connections ought to never be underestimated. When links are set up, they should be sustained continually. No one is impeccable. Expecting flawlessness is setting yourself up for frustration.

Amicable Cooperation

It is hard to make progress without the amicable collaboration of others. A satisfying character is adaptable and versatile while looking after levelheadedness. Adaptability doesn't mean unstable or defenseless behavior.

It implies surveying and reacting correctly and in a promising way to a given circumstance. Flexibility doesn't stretch to standards and qualities.

Show Empathy

An inappropriate we do to other people and what we endure is weighed unexpectedly. Sympathy alone is a significant quality of a constructive character. Individuals with compassion pose themselves this inquiry: "How might I feel on the off chance that somebody treated me that way?"

A puppy

A kid went to the pet store to purchase a little dog. Four of them were sitting together, estimated at $50 each. At that point, there was one sitting alone in a corner. The kid inquired as to whether that was from a similar litter, on the off chance that it was available to be purchased, and why it was sitting alone. The storekeeper answered that it was from a similar litter; it was a twisted one, and not available to be purchased. The kid asked what the disfigurement was. The storekeeper answered that the little dog was conceived without a hip attachment and had a leg missing. The kid asked, "What will you do with this one?"

The answer was it would be put to rest. The kid inquired as to whether he could play with that young doggie. The storekeeper stated, "Sure." The kid lifted the little dog, and the young doggie licked him on the ear. Quickly the kid concluded that was the doggie he needed to purchase. The storekeeper said, "That isn't available to be purchased!" The kid demanded.

The storekeeper concurred. The kid hauled out $2 from his pocket and raced to get $48 from his mom. As he arrived at the entryway, the storekeeper yelled after him, "I don't comprehend why you would pay full cash for this one when you could purchase a decent one at a similar cost." The kid didn't let out the slightest peep. He lifted his left pant leg, and he was wearing a prop. The pet storekeeper stated, "I get it. Proceed, take this one." This is compassion.

Be Sympathetic

At the point when you share the distress, it partitions; when you share joy, it increases.

WHAT IS THE DIFFERENCE BETWEEN INSPIRATION AND MOTIVATION?

I run classes globally, and individuals frequently inquire as to whether I can inspire others. My answer is no; I can't. Individuals persuade themselves. What I can do, nonetheless, is move them to propel themselves. We can make a helpful domain which can be satisfying. To move individuals to spur themselves, we have to comprehend their needs and needs. There is an immediate connection be tween's inspiration and profitability. Individuals who do only enough to get by so they don't get terminated will never be relevant to any association.

Motivation is evolving thinking; inspiration is an evolving activity. Inspiration resembles fire, except if you continue adding fuel to it, it bites the dust. Much the same as exercise and nourishment don't keep going long; neither does inspiration. Notwithstanding, if the wellspring of inspiration is faith in internal qualities, it turns out to belong- -enduring. What is the best spark? Is it cash? Acknowledgment? Improvement in our satisfaction? Support by those we love? All of these can be inspiring powers. Experience has demonstrated that individuals will do a great deal for cash, more for a decent pioneer, and do most for a conviction. We see this event consistently everywhere throughout the world. Individuals will pass on for a sentence. My goal is to share the way that when we accept that we are liable for our lives and our behavior, our viewpoint toward life improves.

LET'S REDEFINE MOTIVATION

The following intelligent inquiry is, what is an inspiration? Inspiration is something that supports activity or feeling. To spur intends to support and motivate. Inspiration can likewise mean to turn on or light the inclination or movement. Inspiration is amazing. It can convince, persuade, and drive you vigorously. Inspiration can be characterized as rationale inactivity. It is a power that can completely change you.

For what reason do we have to get persuaded? Motivation is the main thrust in our lives. It originates from a craving to succeed. Without progress, there is little pride throughout everyday life; no delight or energy at work and home. Frequently life becomes like an unbalanced wheel giving a bumpy ride. The best foe of inspiration is lack of concern. Lack of interest prompts dissatisfaction, and when individuals are baffled, they surrender since they can't recognize what is significant.

INSPIRATION - HOW DOES IT WORK?

When you comprehend the rule that spurs the spark, you can continue to accomplish your objective and can propel others as well. Your interior inspiration is your drive and frame of mind. It is infectious. The mentality is the way to getting the reaction you need from others. How does an individual remain roused and centered? One significant device that has been utilized by competitors for quite a while is called autosuggestion. Auto recommendations are specific announcements made in the current state and rehashed normally. It is sure, self-talk. Inspiration is ordered into two sorts: outside and inside.

OUTER MOTIVATION

Outer inspiration originates from outside, for example, cash, cultural endorsement, distinction, or dread. Instances of outside inspiration are dread of getting hit by guardians and fear of getting terminated at work. An organization needed to set up a benefits plan. All together for the arrangement to be introduced, it required 100% interest. Everybody joined, except John. The method appeared well and good and was in

The wellbeing of everybody. John, not marking, was the main deterrent. John's director and other associates had attempted to convince him without progress. The proprietor of the organization called John into his office and stated, "John, here is a pen, and these are the papers for you to sign to enlist into the annuity plan. If you don't select, you are terminated this moment." John transferred ownership of right.

The proprietor asked John for what reason he hadn't marked before. John answered, "Nobody clarified the arrangement very as obviously as you did."

Dread Motivation

The upsides of dread inspiration are:

- It takes care of business rapidly.
- It is immediate.
- It avoids misfortune by fulfilling time constraints.
- In the short run, the individual's exhibition may improve.

Execution Goes Up

It isn't phenomenal to see the prey defeating the predator since one is running for its nourishment and the other for its life. We gain from history that slaves worked the pyramids. They must be continually watched and condemned for nonperformance.

The drawbacks of dread inspiration are:

- It is outside, which implies the motivation is there while the help is there. At the point when the inspiration goes, the inspiration additionally goes.
- It causes pressure. Execution is restricted to consistence.
- In the since quite a while ago run, execution goes down. It demolishes imagination.
- They become accustomed to the stick and afterward need a more fabulous stick.

A client asked a worker, "When did you start working here?" He answered, "As far back as they took steps to terminate me."

Motivator Motivation

Outside inspiration can likewise appear as motivating forces, rewards, commission, acknowledgment, and so forth. What are the benefits of motivator inspiration? The significant bit of leeway is that it can work very well as long as the motivation is sufficient. Think about a jackass with a carrot dangling in front and with a truck behind. Impetus inspiration will possibly work if the jackass is hungry enough, the carrot is sweet enough, and the heap is light enough.

Once in a while, you must give the jackass a chance to take a chomp of the carrot; else, it will get debilitated. After the jackass takes a nibble, its stomach is full, and you have to trust that the jackass will get ravenous again before it pulls the truck. This is regularly found in our business condition. The minute sales reps meet their standard; they quit working. This is because their inspiration is constrained to meeting their portion. That is outer, not interior.

WE ARE ALL MOTIVATE EITHER POSITIVELY OR NEGATIVELY

I heard an account of two siblings. One was a medication fiend and an alcoholic who, much of the time, beat up his family. The other one was a fruitful representative who was regarded in the public eye and had a great family. A few people needed to discover why two siblings from similar guardians, raised in the same domain, could be so extraordinary. The first was asked, "Why you do what you do? You are a medication someone who is addicted, an alcoholic, and you beat your family. What inspires you?" He stated, "My dad." They asked, "Shouldn't something be said about your dad?" The answer was, "My dad was a medication someone who is addicted, an alcoholic, and he beat his family. What do you anticipate that I should be? That is the thing that I am." They went to the sibling who was doing everything right and asked him a similar inquiry. "Why you are doing everything. What is your wellspring of inspiration?" And think about what he said?

"My dad. At the point when I was a young man, I used to see my father alcoholic and accomplishing all inappropriate things. I decided that that isn't what I needed to be." Both were inferring their quality and inspiration from a similar source, however one was utilizing it entirely and the other adversely.

Negative inspiration carries the craving to take a more straightforward way, which winds up being the harder way.

VARIOUS THINGS MOTIVATE DIFFERENT PEOPLE

Interior inspiration originates from inside, for example, pride, a feeling of accomplishment, duty, and conviction.

There was a little fellow who used to want standard practice, however, regularly played in the stores and never made it to the soccer eleven. While he was rehearsing, his dad used to sit at the far end, sitting tight for him. The matches had begun, and for four days, he didn't appear for training or the quarter or elimination rounds. Out of the blue, he looked for the finals, went to the mentor, and stated, "Mentor, you have constantly kept me in the stores and never let me play in the finals. In any case, today, if you don't mind, let me play."

The mentor stated, "Child, I'm heartbroken, I can't let you. There are preferable players over you, what's more, it is the finals, the notoriety of the school is in question, and I can't take a risk." The kid argued, "Mentor, I guarantee I won't let you down. I ask of you; it would be ideal if you allowed me to play." The mentor had never observed the kid argue like this previously. He stated, "alright, child, go, play. In any case, I recall that I am conflicting with my better judgment, and the notoriety of the school is in question. Try not to allow me to down." The game began, and the kid played like a house ablaze. Each time he got the show on the road, he shot an objective. He was the best player and the star of the game. His group had a remarkable success.

At the point when the game completed, the mentor went up to him and stated, "Child, how might I have been so off-base in my life. I have never observed you play this way. What was the deal? How could you play so well?" The kid answered, "Mentor, my dad is watching me today." The mentor pivoted and took a gander at where the kid's dad used to sit. There was nobody there. He stated, "Child, your dad used to stay there when you wanted to practice, yet I don't see anybody there today." The kid answered, "Mentor, there is something I never let you know. My dad was visually impaired. Only four days prior, he kicked the bucket. Today is the first day he is watching me from above."

Interior motivation

Inside inspiration is the inward satisfaction, not for progress or winning, yet for the joy that originates from having done it. It is an inclination of achievement, instead of merely accomplishing an objective. Arriving at a disgraceful goal doesn't give a satisfying preference. Inward inspiration is enduring because it originates from inside and converts into self-motivation. Motivation should be distinguished and continually reinforced to succeed.

Keep your objectives before you and read them morning and night. The two most significant propelling variables are acknowledgment and obligation. Acceptance implies being valued, being treated with deference and nobility, and feeling a feeling of having a place. Commitment gives an individual sentiment of having a home and possession. He, at that point, turns out to be a piece of the master plan. The absence of duty can become demotivating. Financial rewards are transitory and brief; they are not satisfying over the long haul.

Conversely, seeing a thought being actualized can be sincerely satisfying without anyone else's input. Individuals feel they are not being dealt with like items. They think some portion of a beneficial group. The reward of making the best choice independent from anyone else is persuading.

THE FOUR STAGES FROM MOTIVATION TO DEMOTIVATION

Spurred Ineffective

When is a representative generally spurred in the cycle of business? At the point when he joins an association. Why? Since he needs to demonstrate that by procuring him, the company settled on the correct choice. He is propelled, but since he is new to the earth, he doesn't have a clue what to do. So he is incapable. This is the phase when the worker is most liberal, open, and simple to form to the way of life of the association.

Preparing and direction become basic. Amateurish associations have none or indigent direction programs. On the first day at work, the boss shows the new representative of his work environment and guides him and leaves. He explains all the terrible alongside the decency that he is doing. The new representative rapidly adapts every one of the missteps the chief is making since that is the thing that he has been instructed. The association loses the chance to shape the person to the way of life of that association. Proficient associations, then again, take extreme care to accept individuals into their associations.

They disclose to them, in addition to other things, the accompanying:

- The chain of importance
- Desires for one another
- Do's and doughnuts
- Parameters and rules
- What is worthy and what isn't
- What are the assets

How might one expect execution except if desires are clarified forthright? On the off chance that acceptance and direction are progressed admirably, numerous potential issues would not surface by any means.

Spurred Effective

This is the phase when the worker has realized what to do and does it with drive and vitality. He has taken in the exchange, and it reflects in his presentation. At that point he proceeds onward to the following stage.

Demotivated Effective

After some time, the inspiration level goes down, and the worker begins learning the little-known techniques. This is the phase when the representative isn't roused. He keeps doing simply enough with the goal that the business has no motivation to fire him, yet he isn't roused. This stage is inconvenient to development - the vast majority in associations fall into this third stage. A persuaded proficient learns the exchange and leaves the secrets to cheats and evildoers, however a demotivated worker begins attacking the organization. His presentation is minimal. He ridicules the great entertainers. He dismisses new thoughts and spreads the pessimism all around. Our goal is to take them back to the second phase of persuaded dynamic through preparing. A representative should not to remain in the third organize excessively long; in light of the fact that from here it is possible that they move back to the subsequent stage, which is being roused and dynamic, or they move into the fourth arrange.

Demotivated Ineffective

At this stage, the business doesn't have a lot of decision yet to terminate the representative, which might be the most proper activity at any rate now. Keep in mind, businesses need a similar something as workers do. They need to succeed and improve business, and in the event that representatives help in this goal, at that point they make themselves important and make their progress.

DEMOTIVATING FACTORS

A portion of the demotivates are:

- Unfair analysis
- Negative analysis
- Public mortification
- Rewarding the nonperformer which can be demotivating for the entertainer
- Failure or dread of disappointment
- The achievement which prompts lack of concern
- Lack of bearing
- Lack of quantifiable goals
- Low confidence
- Lack of needs
- Negative self-talk
- Office legislative issues
- Unfair treatment
- Hypocrisy
- Poor benchmarks
- Frequent change
- Responsibility without power

A fulfilled individual isn't really a persuaded individual. A few people are content with practically nothing. For this situation, fulfillment may prompt smugness.

Inspiration originates from fervor, and energy doesn't occur except if there is full responsibility. New strategies for inspiration won't work until the demotivating factors are expelled. Ordinarily, simply evacuating the demotivating elements can start inspiration.

Helpers

What we need to achieve is self-inspiration, when individuals get things done for their reasons and not yours. That is an enduring inspiration. Keep in mind, the most brilliant helper is conviction. We need to show ourselves that we are liable for our activities and behavior. At the point when individuals acknowledge duty, everything improves quality, profitability, connections, and collaboration. A couple of steps to inspire others:

- Give acknowledgment
- Give regard
- Make work intriguing
- Be a decent audience
- Throw a test
- Help yet don't accomplish for others what they ought to accomplish for themselves

Individuals get things done for their reasons, not yours. A tale about Ralph Waldo Emerson outlines this. He and his child used to be attempting to get a calf into the horse shelter. Both father and child were depleted, pulling, and pushing. A young lady was cruising by, and she sweetly put her little finger into the calf's mouth, and the calf affectionately pursued her to the horse shelter.

ACTIVITY PLAN

1. Build up a feeling of pride through preparing.
2. Reward execution.
3. Set well-characterized, clear objectives.
4. Set elevated requirements.
5. Set clear, quantifiable benchmarks.
6. Assess the necessities of others.
7. Make others part of your enormous picture. Set a genuine model by being a positive good example. Fabricate the confidence of others.

CONCLUSION

All in all, we are altogether destined to have fruitful existences, however our molding drives us to disappointment. We are destined to win however are molded to lose. We regularly hear explanations like, this individual is simply fortunate, he contacts the earth, and it goes to gold or, he is unfortunate, regardless of what he feels, it goes to tidy. This isn't valid. On the off chance that you break down, the effective individual is accomplishing something directly in every exchange, and the disappointment is rehashing a similar slip-up in every deal.

Keep in mind, practice doesn't make impeccable. Just flawless careful discipline brings about promising results. Practice makes perpetual whatever you over and again do. A few people continue rehearsing their slip-ups, and they become flawless in them. So their slip-ups become total and programmed. Experts make things look simple since they have aced the essentials of whatever they do. Numerous individuals do great work considering advancements. Yet, the one to whom great work turns into a habit is meriting. Developing a training resembles furrowing the field. It requires some investment. It needs to develop from inside. Examples create different habits.

Motivation is the thing that kicks an individual off; inspiration is the thing that keeps him on track, and practice is the thing that makes it programmed. The capacity to show fortitude even with difficulty; show poise notwithstanding allurement; pick bliss in the front of hurt; show character despite despair; see opportunity even with impediments. These qualities are not fortuitous events; they are the consequence of steady and reliable preparing, both mental and physical.

Despite difficulty, our behavior must be the one we have drilled, paying little respect to whether it is certain or negative. At the point when we practice negative attributes, for example, weakness or deceptive nature in little occasions, planning to deal with the significant ones decidedly, the last won't occur on the grounds that that isn't what we have rehearsed.

At the point when we license ourselves to lie once, it is significantly simpler to do it a second and a third time until it turns into a habit. Achievement lies in the way of thinking of support and avoid. Support what should be done and refuse what is impeding until this gets habitual. Individuals are more passionate than discerning. Genuineness and uprightness are both the aftereffect of our conviction framework and practice.

Anything we practice long enough gets imbued into our arrangement and turns into a habit. An individual who is straightforward more often than not gets captured the first occasion when he tells an untruth. While an individual who is exploitative more often than not gets found the first occasion when, he comes clean. Genuineness and untrustworthiness to self as well as other people both become habits. Our reasoning example gets habitual. We structure habits and habits to manufacture character. Before you understand

That you have the habit, the habit has got you. We have to frame the practice of reasoning right. Somebody once stated, "Our considerations lead to activities, activities lead to habits, and habits structure character." Character prompts predetermination.

www.ingramcontent.com/pod-product-compliance
Lightning Source LLC
Chambersburg PA
CBHW030645220526
45463CB00004B/1650